UNकही:
Buffering Beyond the Barrel
Anthology of Prose and Poems from the Indian Armed Forces

*UN*कही:
Buffering Beyond the Barrel
Anthology of Prose and Poems from the Indian Armed Forces

Compiled and Edited by

Dr. Pragya Bajpai & Lt Col Salil Jain

Highbrow Scribes Publications
New Delhi

*Un*कही
Buffering Beyond the Barrel
*Anthology of Prose and Poems from
the Indian Armed Forces
Dr. Pragya Bajpai & Lt Col Salil Jain*

Published 2024 by Highbrow Scribes Publications
Printed in New Delhi, India

ISBN: 978-81-956557-6-2

Highbrow Scribes Publications's mission is to foster a universal
passion for reading by partnering with authors to help create stories
and communicate ideas that inform, entertain, and inspire, and to
connect them with readers everywhere.

Highbrow Scribes Publications books are printed on acid-free paper.

www.highbrowscribes.com

Dedicated to

The Unsung life of Indian Defence Forces,
their Family and the loved ones.

Contents

Foreword   xi
Preface   xiii
Acknowledgements   xv

ENGLISH

Abhishek Kumar Singh   1
Anita Panda   2
Ankita Srivastava   5
Ashwani Sharma   8
Ashwini R Sane   10
Avinash SN   13
Arti Chopra   16
Aaryaman Suryavanshi   19
Balachandran Nair   20
Charu Kalra   22
Deepti Menon   26
Dilip Mohapatra   28
Gaurav Bhatia   32
GD Bakshi   35
Gopal Purdhani   37
Harnoor Grewal   39
Itika Kahlon Virk   43
Jhanvi   45

JK Bhagwat 47

Jyotirmoy Ghosal 49

Ketaki Pimplekhare 53

Krishna Kumar 55

Kumud Mishra 57

Lily Swarn 60

Monisha Rastogi 63

Nandita De Nee Chatterjee 67

Navdeep Multani 69

Navneet Grewal 72

Paromita Mukherjee Ojha 76

Pragya Bajpai 82

Pravin Raghuvanshi 86

Priya Khanna 90

Raj Krushna Mishra 92

Reena Singh 93

Renuka Shukla 96

Roopali Sircar Gaur 99

Rupa Rao 104

Sahana Ahmed 108

Sanjeev Sethi 110

Seema Ahira 112

Shyamola Khanna 115

Siddhant Kaushal 120

Sujata Parashar 122

Sunil Kaushal   123

Swati Pal   127

Tanushree Poddar   129

Toolika Rani   133

Tulika Niyogi   137

Vidisha Kaushal   140

Vandana Parashar   142

Vinita Narula   144

Vivek Kamthan   148

हिन्दी

आर्या कुमारी   155

अभिषेक आनंद त्रिपाठी   157

अभ्युदय प्रकाश   160

आदित्य देशमुख   164

आदित्य पवार   165

आकांक्षा मोदानी   167

अखिलेश यादव   169

अनीता शर्मा   171

डी वी संतोष मेहेर   173

गौतम नांद्रेकर   175

गोपाल पुरधानी   177

हरीश जोशी   178

इन्दु तोमर	180
इंदु वशिष्ठ	182
जितेन्द्र सिंह	183
ममता पंडित	184
नित्या शुक्ला	186
पियूष शर्मा	189
प्रज्ञा बाजपेयी	192
प्रवेश धायल	193
पूजा अत्री	195
रमा शर्मा	198
रंजीता सहाय अशेष	202
सलिल जैन	204
श्याम सुन्दर शर्मा	207
सुखदीप सांगवान	209
सुशील दत्त 'देव'	211
वर्षा रानी	213
वन्दना यादव	215
विनोद कुमार पंत	218
यासीन मोहम्मद	221

FOREWORD

It gives me immense pleasure to write a foreword for a unique endeavour that unites poets and authors, hailing from the military fraternity, showcasing panache in literary expression, besides their combat skills. The compilation is not just a collection of prose and poems, but a reflection across a wide spectrum of experiences and emotions, that will captivate readers.

This effort, to provide a common platform to poets and authors from the Armed Forces fraternity in sharing their literary flourish, is truly commendable. The wide array of experiences put forth by poets and authors delving into history and culture of our great nation, is bound to leave the readers enthralled as well as inspired.

My compliments to the Editorial Team for bringing out a fine compilation of rich and thought provoking works. I wish 'Unkahi : Buffering Beyond The Barrels' team success, in future endeavours.

'Jai Hind'

(Manoj Pande)
General
Chief of the Army Staff

Preface

Unkahi was initiated as an independent house of conditioned minds born in and around the fraternity of Indian warriors with an aim of uniting the creative writers across the nation. The first collection of poems from the house called **Unkahi: The Unsung** (2021) was curated to nestle the poetic space for the muse of veterans and young officers alike. It was successfully able to spread its influence and inspiration across the national fabric among the tri-services.

The second volume, **Unkahi: Buffering Beyond the Barrel** has breathed a new life into the archived leaves from the diaries of multiple writers and poets. It is a jewel of creative writings embedded with organic thoughts, spiritual interventions, episodes of flirting with destiny, touching narratives, fond memories, training immersions, proud moments, excerpts from curated conversations, memoirs, lifestyle stories and poetic reminiscences of the metaphysics of what it takes to stay committed to a cause; and the cause is nothing but one's own motherland. It is a feeble attempt to unravel fighters' inner life and reflections in any form that twinkles between reality and imagination.

The **Unkahi** platform has gradually turned into an engaging ode to the human emotions in uniform, the enigma behind immaculate appearances and inherent art that lies in the nurtured moments of border and beyond; all that is intangible and unfathomable to the world outside the garrison and guarded premise. It has grown and prospered by leaps and bounds since 2021.

It was a privilege to compile and edit the collection brimming with hope, love, dedication and nostalgia that seamlessly connects and conveys authentic feelings of a brave league. Through their raw emotions and genuine expressions, the poets salute the national flag fluttering proudly on the independent mother land.

Jai Hind!

Editors

Acknowledgements

We are extremely grateful to the esteemed General Manoj Pande, PVSM, AVSM, VSM, ADC, Chief of Army Staff (COAS) for graciously writing an overwhelming foreword for the book that adds an extra charm to the anthology. We wholeheartedly thank him for his inspiring words and constant motivation. We sincerely thank Lt Col Vivek Tripathi serving at ADG PI for all the support and guidance.

We also express our deepest gratitude to all the poets for making this endeavour successful by sending their creations. Without their magical poetry, this journey wouldn't have been possible.

Special thanks to **Highbrow Scribes Publications** for meticulously turning this dream into a reality.

Yours Truly,
Dr. Pragya Bajpai & Lieutenant Colonel Salil Jain
Editors
editorsanthology@gmail.com

English

Abhishek Kumar Singh

Running In The Rain

Sometimes meaningful
Sometimes in vain
Running in the rain
I witnessed
Clouds came closer to the earth
And simply kissed

It's like touching the
Natures grace first hand
It's like touching the cheeks
As loose sand

It's like witnessing the
Emotions of the cloud
Sometimes silent
And sometimes loud

Dressed in black coming to meet
Her lady dressed in brown
Putting the droplets as pearls
And greenery all around

Though far off can't actually reach
My love my lady
My love for you is
Defined by the droplets each

Anita Panda

Soldiers Never Die...

"Is life as beautiful as the fresh little dew?

That glides over the juvenile, naked leaf?

Or, is it as gruesome as the marauding cells?

Briefly halted by the surgeon's cold steel?

Fight, O' brave One! Fight!' -Surya Panda-

As a little boy, he loved to play with the Army toy tank gifted to him by our Father. That sowed early within him the seeds to be an aspiring soldier and nurtured his fierce ambition to join the armed forces. He achieved his dream and commissioned as a Captain in the Indian Army in 1989, passing out as a proud cadet of the prestigious IMA, Dehradun.

From the icy Kargil heights to the beautiful woods of J&K, the humid jungles of the North-East to the scorching deserts of Thar, he fought each counter-insurgency operation on India's borders as valiantly as the invisible enemy lurking within. Detected with lethal 'Malignant Melanoma' cancer in 2018, in his superannuation year, he battled the monster with supreme positivity and heroic courage! Unfazed and undaunted. "The end will come when it has to," he would say calmly, stoically braving the rounds of painful chemos.

Surya was a Warrior! Years of gruelling military training had taught him to meet his demons head-on and view his critical illness "as a great learning in pain management." Giving up was not an option for him! He fought each challenge life threw at him with robust courage and positivity few could match. His words- 'Keep the soldier in you alive always," invited as a guest speaker at Fortis, Noida, on World Cancer Day resonate his 'never-say-die' attitude! Receiving a thunderous applause both for his uplifting speech as well as for earning his MBA degree from IIM Lucknow at the convocation, barely a month-and-a-half post his critical six hours surgery on Nov 13, 2018. He was a real-life HERO!

A die-hard patriot, an award-winning poet- awarded 'Poet of the Year' by the 'Poet's International Organisation' for his poem 'War & Peace' (1983), an ace athlete, adventurist, mature thinker and a zesty cricketer, Surya played friendly matches against eminent cricketers- Mohammed Azharuddin & Dilip Doshi and in the Kolkata First division cricket league in school. A gifted actor and director of plays at school and college, Surya declined a lead role in a tele-serial with talented actor Pallavi Joshi in the 80's, given his passion for the Indian Army. He represented the Indian Army at the International Hot air balloon contest in 1990.

A man of exceptional strength and courage! Amongst his many achievements and in a dare-devil feat, Surya was instrumental in bringing down a 'sick' Army chopper from a high-altitude glacier down to the base camp in 'Op Vijay', Kargil in '99-2001. One of the two selected officers, he visited Israel in 2006 to master Drone technology in 2006 and actively involved in various military and administrative activities of the Indian Army.

A man of action and compassion. A valiant officer and a fine gentleman. A selfless soul with his gentle and charming smile, Surya touched so many lives in so many ways.

When the end came in the early hours of 9th January, 2021, Surya succumbed but not without one last fierce fight! This brave son of India departed in true military style draped in the tri-colours of the national flag with full military honours and given a glorious gun salute; befitting a true soldier!

I am proud to have compiled and published his rare collection of poems- GENESIS- a sister's heartfelt ode to her brother and a valiant soldier in September 2021. A paean to the unsung poet and thinker who had mastered "wisdom with pain".

Surya, my sibling, confidante, critic, counsellor, mentor was no ordinary human. He lived as bravely as he died. With grit and guts leaving behind a rich legacy and immortal like the brilliant Sun true to his name! He fought and how! Gone from this earthly realm now but ubiquitous in the vast cosmos. He lives on through his indomitable spirit. You fought well and invincibly my Brother! For Soldiers never die! JAI HIND!

Ankita Srivastava
The Lion And The Lamb

She, I thought was a big lion

When I was told to escort her as a lamb

Her fun trip up the curves of the eastern sector was planned carefully

I sat quiet all through watching her from the corners of my eyes occasionally

She binged on the sandwiches that were kept as per her taste buds

Not offering me even once coz she assumed I didn't have any taste buds !

She at 40, flirted with the Mirik lake waters dipping her feet,

And she walked in a dancing tune amidst the pine trees

I at 25, stared at all the things

The tourists, The trees, The man-made lake

And one BSF DIG's carcade

She declared the dull water tired her feet

So we started to recede

But some hunters got the news of a lion in an office car

Boulders were lined up in the katcha road as well as on road of coal tar

She wailed and threw her lion's skin aside turning into a lamb

I picked up her skin as I kicked out of me my own little lamb

I was out of the car
Frog leaping towards the BSF DIG's car
My military I-card shown, my courage unknown

"Allow my car to precede your weapon laden escort vehicle," I said
"at your own risk and peril as applicable," he simply said

Frog leaping back, I ordered the driver to act smart
DIG's car and our car should look like a part
She howled that today she will be kidnapped for sure
I told her to keep quiet as I will save her for sure
She shouted - are you a power puff girl ?
I retorted - I am an Army officer not a girl !

The DIG's vehicle came closer
I directed the driver to manoeuvre
We were soon moving at highest speed possible
Each Gorkhali kept standing with his sharp weapon
While our car crossed the hells and reached the safe haven.

Life Is A Summersault

You came with your noisy footsteps
And showed me your heels are much higher than mine
I gaped at you mesmerised, walking past me
Though I noticed, you had a borrowed style of an old English wine

I watched you sway and heard you say
"Don't even try to copy me as you just can't do so"
I feigned a smile
And I quietly walked away

Your head started growing up on your narrow shoulders
Till the weight of it started weighing you down
The donkey that you found in me
To your surprise had learnt to gallop around

You added some wings to your clothes
And I was still searching for the glue
You were about to fly
When it was me who actually flew!!!

Ashwani Sharma

The Wooden Bridge

The wooden structure of the bridge stands tall
The story of two states, it tells all
The two ends of bridge are two different domains
One is radiant, immune to all pains
The other is uneventful, captivated by time
Screaming out the prejudice done, in rhyme
Towards the brighter side there's a mall
The wooden structure of the bridge stands tall.

Carts moving by make the dust rise high
Metalled roads, highways and expressways make the ply
Future of Bharat learning in the dark
India's productivity touching the benchmark
People towards the Bharat side are in traditional attire
Developed and hi-tech Bharat still a satire
WhatsApp, Facebook, Instagram and 4G call
The wooden structure of the bridge stands tall.

Light coming from the radiant side was bit hazy
In polluting the nature that side was crazy
Dull and uneventful side I chose to go
My perceptions were wrong, it wasn't so
The silence and purity of Bharat was eternal
While in India the battle was internal
Though the length of bridge is getting small
The wooden structure of the bridge stands tall.

The Marvels Of Nature

How splendid the rising sun look
Cannot define its beauty even in a book
Illusionist nature starts its day with the morning mist
Nature's magical show has got a long list
She controls everything, the element and the creature
And puts up the show- THE MARVELS OF NATURE

The handsome sun soon turned hostile
The soft earth became a rock-solid tile
"mercy, o nature", the earth cried
Clouds were called up for the earth dried
The sky was now black full of thunder
To relief the earth from the sun's blunder
It rained heavily to quench the thirst of earth
For coming to rescue with its marvels, the nature had no dearth

The time was for the next show
The rainbow painted by nature came to life quite slow
After painting the canvas, I thought the magician has gone
Nature screamed, "there's more, hold on"
The beautiful red sun was drowning in the horizon against the sky
The colours of rainbow withered but for its survival it gave a last try
Why she was doing such wonders, what was her aim?
She replied "today is not the last day, the show-THE MARVELS OF NATURE will be manifested again.

Ashwini R Sane

The Mosquito's Philosophy

After midnight at half past two,

The cold wind came in and softly flew,

Awake so suddenly, with many thoughts within,

Hair on end, goosebumps on soft skin!

There were many questions in my mind therein;

'Where am I now? Where am I going?

What did I achieve? What had I seen?

What am I doing?

The goals that I had long time back so proudly drawn,

I had achieved not even one!

Oh! What a useless life I lead?

When some of my contemporaries have met success on a steed,

I had a lead, but now I feel stuck with no speed!'

The soft breeze came in and then came a humming in my ear,

Mr. Mosquito was hovering nearby without fear!

'My dear human you are all insane!

You are living a lovely life why complain?

Why this negativity and self-hate?

Look at me I know my fate!

Yet I fly on every day and every night very late!

People like you are my sweet bait!

A second I am lazy, it will be too late!

I have no time to speculate or contemplate!

Yet I live on in this life a circus,

Each one comes here with a purpose,

Maybe, like me just in a moment, you never know, you might have touched some one's

Life, filled it with happiness, removed their misery, their strife

You might never know, and that is how life flows, you may never know,

There are many places you have been to and still shall go!

Didn't you go to the best schools you fool!

Travelled over mountains,

Ate many dishes, met people

And got many warm wishes?

No you haven't yet lost your way,

Tomorrow you are lucky to see the lovely day!

That's my philosophy of life I'm sorry I cannot much stay....

With a small bite,

The mosquito flew away!

Wondering In The Night

Have you ever wondered in the night;
Though the lamp post has the brightest light,
yet the fireflies still glow surreally green?

Have you ever wondered as the moon shines down at night,
How the grey clouds drift in, is it to let the stars shine serene?

Have you ever wondered, as the shadows drop and prance,
Is it the crickets singing to cause them to dance?
The leaves clap their performance in a trance,

Have you ever wondered, what the white owl hoots at night?
Why the hounds howl in the dark?
The frogs croak in twos, I wonder whom he will woo?

Have you ever wondered as the night sets its music tone,
And on you are on your bed alone, you wonder, from all things
come and gone,
The people, your friends, and in all your homes, that
Night was always the same?

Have you ever wondered when
all the night creatures sing in tune,
and you hear the music in your room,
Is their lullaby for you to sleep?
Sleep well, and safely, dream sweet!

Avinash SN

My Coursemate

Little did I know what my life had in store,
when I joined the forces hearing the lore.
I let my soul fly, set my dreams free,
and my life began with a soldier's decree.

I knew I needed this, this way to live by,
for I wasn't made for office or a shirt and tie.
My days in Academy, memories were made,
both good and bad, but never to fade.

Each dawn we rushed with Bugler's call,
together we would rise, together we'd fall.
Not my sibling, not my blood in his vein,
but course mate he was, sharing our pain.

Thicker than thieves, toiling day and night,
we had our backs, each other at sight.
We broke a few rules, our shenanigans,
found new ways and means to have our share of fun.

Soon we earned the sobriquet - weird pair,
the name was not entirely false, as we were.
We were nothing alike - chalk and cheese,
they say opposites attract, if you please.

He was punctual and I was inevitably late,
he stood by me, bonded by fate.
His shoes were shiny, mine were begrimed,
but together we stuck, together we chimed.

Little did we realise how the time passed,
what mattered was the joy we amassed.
Soon it was the day of our passing out,
the day every cadet would dream about.

I was happy, yet foreboding the separation,
soon we'd part ways to serve the nation.
He would don the OG and I, my whites,
playing our roles, fighting our fights.

Eventually was I to learn, about this bond,
that life is an ocean, Academy a pond.
As he joined his regiment and I, my ship,
I feared a possible chasm in our friendship.

Life thus took us on its roller coaster ride,
for a change, I couldn't find him by my side.
Years rolled by and we grew up fast,
our plans to meet, pushed down to the last.

After an eternity, we met by happenstance,
my heart leapt joyfully in a frenzy dance.
We picked it up from right where we left,

we chatted as he drove his car with deft.

We laughed at this strange thing called life,
Both of us settled and each with a wife.
We separated as boys, met as men.
Surprisingly, I spoke less and chose to listen.

Our bond is beyond time and space,
What has changed other than my face?
Years might pass but it's never late,
to relive the memories with a course mate.

Arti Chopra
My Pen

My pen seems to have dried up
The ink has stopped flowing
The blank white paper stares at me
But there is a calm knowing

Hesitantly I begin to write
The thoughts are coming fast
The strength that seems to pervade me
I know is going to last

I will face what life offers
I will be happy, yet at times sad
That is what life is all about
Facing equally the good and the bad

I will not lose myself in pain
My pain will be my cure
The quote above by Rumi
Is a startling truth I'm sure

Everywhere I look is God's love
I'm not alone at all,
Such amazing peace and strength he gives
I'm standing proud and tall

Tribute To My Soldier

No time to say goodbye
No time to feel the pain
Death was so shocking
When unannounced it came

It wasn't anything different
It was our normal day
He got up in the morning
And got ready to go and play

We had had a beautiful dinner
I turned and went to sleep
What made me order his favourite?
I even treated him to a sweet

He went on sending greetings
Late into that awful night
Janmaashtami was the day God chose
For him it was so right

Pure souls just do not suffer
God fulfils their every whim
He left as he had wanted
A vessel of goodness filled to the brim
My world has suddenly tilted
The ground has slipped from beneath my feet

But the ocean of love that surrounds me
Will conquer my defeat

His life will be an inspiration
For his children who he loved so much
He always led by example
There will never be one such

Life always comes full circle
His good deeds shall bear sweet fruit
Pure love is what life is all about
Now I am a tree that lost it root

But peace will keep me grounded
Because God has held my hand
I shall ask he be reborn in India
Because my brave soldier loved his land

Aaryaman Suryavanshi

An Urban Ode

In gleams of the night,
In glares of the sight,
In merries of the rich,
In clinks of the bowl,
I search for you,
To come and find me,
I ask for you,
To come and find me.

I see you glimmer,
Like a star on concrete,
I see you gleam,
Like my moon on the street.
I yearn for your touch,
On the steel cold tiles,
In minutes of the traffic,
Stacked up for miles.

I pray for this city,
And ask it of you,

I lay in this urban,
For I live it for you.
In dusk of the hills,
early smokes of the mills,
In dews of the morn,
Till the mist of the dawn,
I search for you,
To come and find me,
I yearn for you,
To come and find me.

I see you, once again,
Like hope to a befallen,
I see you come near,
Like courage to my fear.
I think of this city,
And I ask it of you,
I loathe this urban,
But I live it for you.

Balachandran Nair

For The First Time

When rising Sun kissed horizon

for a first time

Birds sang, human activities sprang

When butterfly sat on flower

for a first time

It shrivelled in shy and secreted honey.

When military uniform touched my body

for a first time

Patriotism sprouted, duty and responsibility spruced.

When one day, liquor touched

my senses for a first time...

Common sense deserted; humbleness howled

Old age turned astonishingly young

Children all looked like grown-ups

Well-dressed looked like naked

Highways shrinked and narrowed

Earth shivered, crumbled under my foot

Sun, hot, reached out to shake hand

People around spoke strange languages

Predecessors waved from heaven

All those idiots roaming around

sought my help to stand erect

People fell down, buildings rotated,

Myself was the only one straight forward....

So, see guys, I don't have time

to entertain you people, sorry.

But why I too am falling on road now, pee,

My unwilling eyes closing, weeping?

Such a thing happened

Only twice in my life earlier

Once was when SHE kissed me

for a first time!

I forgot my surroundings.

Don't ask me who She is.

It is top secret.

The other once is...

When Starts kissed my shoulder

On pipping ceremony in Indian Military!

I forgot my superiors.

Don't ask me what happened next!

Charu Kalra

Strings Of Solemn Words

Incessant strings of solemn words,
On an imaginative quest for contentment and mirth.
Intertwining threads of quaint verse,
In its folios emotions immerse.

Scads of muddled thoughts and obscured passion,
Suffuse pages with vivid impressions.
Reminiscent strokes of enthralling tales,
Stories spoken and the unknown leave a trail.

In a kaleidoscope of soulful sagas, artistic acumen dwells;
Life's tribulations and tepid waves, it dispels.
Creative urge with incandescent rays,
Unfilled canvas with a smidgeon of hope and faith.

Poignant and boundless notions so profound,
Penchant for painting mosaic images in its cosmic expanse and
beyond.
Empty pages beckon and touch the heart and soul,
Reflections from the snippets enliven and behold.

Enriching boundaries of sole existence,
Wondrous manifestation of poetic credence.
Sharing tears of ecstasy in a lonely lane,
Quill that inscribes the unsaid, is all that remains.

Delving into the mystical world of prose and folklore,

Embarking on infinite alleys of legends, myths, parables and more.

Synapses from life unfold the tapestry of intricate shades,

Traversing in solitude and seeking solace in the pen that creates.

In Its Sacred Shadow:
The Old Tree

Old tree beneath the empyreal sky,

Holding under its canopy nascent life.

Swaying in azure breeze and mystic chimes,

Embracing enchanting nature's rhymes.

Array of fragrant flowers and leaves,

In its redolence buoyant reveries, entwines and weaves.

Soothing and mellifluent sounds,

Whisper vernal hymns all around.

Spring beholds its ethereal magnificence,

Motley of vibrant blossoms sashaying in pure essence.

From the heavens warbling birds alight,

Perkier paths aglow with sprinkles of pristine light.

Embedded roots and tendrils of hope,

Boughs gleam with tints of the summer orb.

Rustling echoes and sultry winds,

Caresses soul with seasons' hints.

Tiny beads amidst the misty lanes,

Euphonic rains and glistening drizzles wither the pain.

Slender twigs and soaked emotions,

Enticing petrichor with deep ruminations.

Wistful autumn paints ether with myriad hues,
Sheds and waits for fresh effervescent blooms.
Ensconcing its bare and unadorned folds,
Continues to stand strong and holds.

Winter nips and sheaths of frost,
Branches swathed in sublime thoughts.
Hazy billows and secluded realms,
It lay resilient in the rugged elms.

Old tree seeks only perseverance,
Promising faith and assurance.
To withstand the abyss and trials of life,
In its sacred shadow all this while.

Deepti Menon

Any More For Any More?

How familiar is this phrase within the Indian Army! Every posting, and there have been quite a few in over thirty years, has come with its share of Tambola mornings/ evenings/ nights, those few minutes of nail-biting tension when breaths are held in anticipation of that one elusive number.

I remember how we would rush across and buy our tickets just so that we could get a comfortable spot, close enough to hear the announcement, but strategically placed even closer to the bar and the snack tables. Drinks all around, boards and pencils distributed and a pregnant pause while the last-minute crowd would buy their tickets, even as the avid players grumbled at the delay.

Dividends would follow. The announcer's voice would cut across. "May I have your attention, please?" and promptly have his attention diverted by a little boy collecting pencils. The dividends would be repeated with a minimum of fuss, but have to be repeated about five times before they were heard over the small talk and the kids' excitement.

The harassed announcer would fortify himself with a stiff drink, reminding the folks around not to disown their particularly noisy little ones. In the hush that ensued, he would quickly begin to call out the numbers, with players telling him to slow down or shake the numbers depending on their expertise at the game.

"Doctor's orders, number nine" followed by "Lucky blind, seventy" would continue as the uninitiated wondered what was so lucky about being blind. The smaller prizes would soon vanish, and the full houses would follow suit. The hush would be offset in a rumble of discontent, all in good fun, of course.

There were people who would win every time round, but

these were rare specimens. The rest would lose all the year around, their hopes bolstered by the popular adage, "Lucky in love, unlucky at Tambola!" Suddenly, a winning spree would come their way and they would do a little jig and collect their winning for the year.

After every house, the gentlemen would get up and replenish their spirits (pun intended!) while the ladies would gorge on the peanuts and onions, the mini egg and toast snack and probably, the dry chicken, if they were lucky enough to catch a glimpse of it. It would normally be polished off by the 'spirited' gentlemen at the bar itself.

After the bumper house, dinner would be announced. The ladies would make a beeline to the counters, hoping against hope that their better halves would also do so. Many a time have many of us reached home, happily satiated, only to find that the early birds had, indeed, caught the worm, and that our husbands were not part of these avian species.

Dinner, of course, would be the standard Army meal of bread and eggs, and if the bachelors followed you home, it would be a whopping meal of the same. Plus, all the leftovers nestling in small containers within the refrigerator, leaving the kitchen looking as though a storm had swept through it.

These encounters had their own charm. They built up bonds of togetherness and were filled with moments of great fun and frolic. None of us ever complained about these midnight raids. Even today, we have a deep association with those very same young officers who raided our homes, and have grown to be senior officers, retired and serving.

That, indeed, is the charm of life in the Armed Services!

Dilip Mohapatra

The Veteran

After his morning walk
around the periphery of his
residential complex
he picks up from his famished letterbox
a crumpled brown envelope
with a familiar rubber stamp
indicating the dispatcher
as Navy Headquarters.

He ambles up the stairs to his apartment
for the elevator is under repairs
and reads out the letter to his wife
with a twinkle in his tired eyes
that no longer he has to
write retired in brackets following his rank
for he now is to be referred
as a Veteran by orders of the
Chief of the Naval Staff.

With his heart filled with pride
he gets ready to join the protest march
of the ex-servicemen demanding
their arrears of pension that are overdue
delayed by the red tape of bureaucracy

and then he has to rush to
the military hospital's special counter
for the retired
to enquire about the insulin
prescribed for him but
unavailable for the last three months.
Then he has to go to the local
elections office to locate his voter's card
that has been going through a process of
serve and volley
for something or the other
the last time with his gender
shown as female
despite his mug shot showing
a well-groomed Van Dyke.

He always finds time
to browse through the posts
of fellow veterans of his WhatsApp group
to read the comments
and counter comments
on almost any topic under the Sun
whether relevant or otherwise
and wonders if really the knight
and the king are equals
inside the box
after the gruelling game is over
on the chessboard

or if the seniority bugs
of all types whether that of
former ranks, age or batch
continue to bite!

His days are long and nights short
and in the small hours
sleep playing hide and seek with his eyes
he sifts his beliefs and re shapes them
with new hopes
to cope with the following day
one day at a time
while he wonders how peacefully he slept
when not on watch
in his bunk swaying with the ship
that rolled pitched and yawed
in tune with the frequency
of the vagrant waves
and how he triangulated the enemy sub
despite the feeble sonar pings
when on midnight watch.

Tomorrow is At Home
with the governor of the state for
The Republic Day celebrations
and he is a special invitee to meet
the American ambassador
an ex-US Marine
and who has asked specifically for him

for they did the war course together
at Annapolis Naval Academy
years ago.

He asks his wife to find the rusty
miniature medals and an old bottle of Brasso
that still languishes in some corner
and sits down with a brush and polish
to spit shine his old black boots.

Gaurav Bhatia

Perseverantia: A Sestina'of Tenacity

In moments dark, a light shines from within,
A magic cherished, solace it bestows,
Uplifting souls, embracing them with grace,
A steadfast beacon in the midst of crisis,
When hope seems lost, it whispers, "Carry On",
Believe in life, in fighting, and in love.

In every heart, this precious gift of love,
A spark that glows, a fire that burns within,
A force that says, "Don't waver, Carry On",
A balm that soothes, a healing touch bestows,
When doubts arise, when faced with the crisis,
It stands unwavering, providing grace.

The "Tenacious Theophile" embraces grace,
And finds the strength to rise again with love,
In every battle faced, in every crisis,
A warrior's spirit burns brightly within,
For deep inside, the magic still bestows
The power to stand tall and "Carry On".

Though shadows fall, I must "Carry On",
With fortitude, to weather storms with grace,
This mystical force of hope it bestows,

Infusing hearts with courage and with love,
Through trials and tribulations deep within,
A resolute resolve emerges from crisis.
In retrospect, we realize, in crisis,
This force was there, urging us, "Carry On,"
Through trials endured, resilience within,
It held us close, enwrapped us with its grace,
A guardian angel, filled with boundless love,
A celestial light, it constantly bestows.

This wondrous magic that the universe bestows,
Is ever-present, even in the crisis,
A constant presence, guiding us with love,
Impelling us to persevere, to "Carry On",
With open hearts, we welcome its sweet grace,
And find the strength to face what lies within.

So, cherish deep within, what's kept within,
The gift of magic that the world bestows,
Embrace its power, its undeniable grace,
A steadfast ally, even through the crisis,
In every heartbeat, it spurs us, "Carry On",
A force of nature, everlasting love.

In every soul, the essence of true love,
Resides this magic, cherished deep within,
Through ups and downs, it whispers, "Carry On",
A gift from above, a blessing it bestows,

In every moment, even in the crisis,
It fills our hearts with hope and boundless grace.

So, in the darkest moments, find the grace,
And know that you are worthy of this love,
With magic in your heart, face every crisis,
For strength resides within, deep down within,
And with its power, endure what life bestows,
With unwavering faith, continue to "Carry On".

Note: *The Sestina is a complex French verse form which usually features unrhymed lines of poetry. It has six sestets, and an ending tercet. The ending words of each line from the first stanza are repeated in a different order as ending words in each of the subsequent five stanzas. The closing tercet contains all six of these ending words, two per line, and they are placed in the middle and at the end of these three lines.*

GD Bakshi

Poems published in his debut poetry collection,
Dances with the Shamans *(1998)*

The Void That Swallows

The great voids
Swallows
those who done alone
far away from home
is this wilderness
of Rock and ice .
The essence of their beings
is swallowed
up by the sun
one by one
each element
returns whence
it come.
Only the light in the eyes
of the Shaman
burns on
As a beacon
for all mankind

Mushrooms Of The Harvest Moon

Let us pluck
the mushrooms
when the moon
is full
when the lymph
of its magic light
sets them all alight
when the fulgor
of its due

will renew
our tired spirits
pieces of the harvest
moon
fall silently to this earth
and become
the magic mushrooms
That opens the gates
of eternal tranquillity

Gopal Purdhani

My Nation Is My Problem

I am an Army Veteran and have crossed 80 years of my age and become a super senior citizen. My other Army Veteran colleagues living in the same or nearby localities have devised a unique method for passing of time that is interesting and has a purpose too.

Generally, we pick up a current national problem and indulge in humorous discussions or debates to reach at a suitable solution.

One of us becomes the victim on behalf of the general public and the other becomes the government official whom we think is responsible for that problem.

Yesterday, I was 5 minutes late, at our usual time and place of meeting in the district Park.

Finding me coming, my friend, retired C Yadav, shouted at me, "Have you forgotten all norms of Army discipline; you late comer, useless bugger."

"These words suit more on you, old man. Except today that I got late due to your fault, You traffic inspector sahib. You people should perform your duties some time, at least. There is a big jam at the crossings and looks like that all traffic police-walas are on leave," I replied.

"I think you public-walas also should learn some road manners and obey traffic rules and above all what are you telling, you are a Neta ji, you have no duty to perform, except sleeping during your normal time of Vidhan Sabha meetings," he retorted back.

I purposely did not respond to that remark but who could stop my friend and he added, "any way that is your unchangeable bad habit, so leave that but tell me what are you doing about changing your culture". He said, "What culture? Why should we change our culture you uneducated dumb?"

"I am talking about culture of corruption. The amount of regular monthly emoluments, multiple pensions, privileges, facilities and what not. It has become deep rooted in the blood of bad characters. Better do something fast. The public has become much wiser now. You cannot keep Robbing them forever".

"I don't know that, Sir!" I shot back my last and final dialogue at him, "Let us go to the bar for glass of beer, you young man." That used to be our favourite phrase to end a discussion. And we proceeded to our favourite resort.

Harnoor Grewal
Call Me Then

Call me then when the hate has ended
When the anger has demolished
And the greedy have become
Mature and polished

Call me then when the pollution is over
When there's no disease
And no suffer moreover

Call me then when there are no widows
No orphans no poor
When the ego has been calmed
And everyone stops being cruel

Call me then when they stop invading
Polluting deteriorating our nature
Damaging and spoiling its stature

Call me then when the color apartheid
Is no more
The law of humanity changes
And doesn't remain abhor
The concrete jungles shout
Emphasizing on the imprudence all about

That falls from far above
With no compassion or love

This wasn't the future
We all foresaw
This wasn't the idea
Implanted in our jaw

Humans we are
Then why has humanity been forgotten?
Trapped in a jar
Thrown in the dump, left to be rotten

I try and try to find
Empathy and sympathy together in a bind
But it has been eroded
Eroded from our hearts
Leaving us scarred

So, let's have faith in each other
Let's not cower
Let's feed the love and not the ego
Let us come together
And speak humanity
In a way it has never been before

Dear India

To me you are more than these lies
More than these flying rumors
More than these false accusations
Or inhuman activities

Every time I walk by you
There is an urge to explore
Desperation to know
The story behind these walls
Of sacrifice and ethos

You emit purity in every way
Your myriad hues bedazzle me
Captivate me in a way no one has

Through the caves, Ghats, rivers
Shrines, mountains and plains
You amplify beauty
In your majestic strains

Your holy beliefs
And the terrain of the sacred
Contradict the toxicity
Written in your name
Your enchanting faith
Leaves me spellbound

The undying hope
The people procure
Gives me yet another
Reason to stay

The *kumbh ka mela*, the *tapri wali chai*
The sacred temples, the busy streets of Delhi
And much more to identify

How shall I describe you in words?
You have always found a way
To alter the amiss
But dear India,
You are so much more than just this!

Itika Kahlon Virk

My Heart N My Soul

There's a place in my heart
So warm and tender
That renders love whole, with no part
And always a known sender

That place has been yours for years 10 now
Sweetly smiling and sparkling, loving and giving
So much you would mean to me, I wonder, how
To be easy and carefree, from you I am learning

My first glance at you, and your first smile
Your first clinch at my fingers, and my overwhelming
'T'was a promise that we be friends, not deterred by any mile
With time what grew closer and stronger has been our bonding
Your first step to your first jump

From your first scribble to your first sentence
I have seen you grow, nicely facing any bump
Never letting a milestone be missed from my lens

From the adorable cute little bundle of joy that you were
You have grown into a fun loving mischievous young girl
From the love you had for all things with fur
You have learnt to appreciate even a ringlet without a curl
Now as you enter the second decade of your life

I'd like to share some valuable advice
It's best to altogether avoid a silly strife
Than to point in the other a usual vice

Make new friends, meet them daily
But if any upsets you, do not take it to heart
For where love binds a relation truly
It will ensure that people do not part

Games and sports keep you active
But never lose focus from your books
Coz they also teach you to be wisely selective
Whenever you happen to deal with any of the crooks

Develop a hobby, master it too
For you'll feel happy when acknowledged
Be it singing, writing or creating without glue
Appreciate the plants, birds and even fabrics with no selvedge

Imbibe all goodness that you come across
Ignore the evil, hoping it shall never befall
Helping humanity is a part of all things gross
And always pay heed to your inner call

This is, my darling, your mum's heartfelt emotion
Just tried to pen down all that I could and should
You are God's absolutely wonderful and intelligent creation
Never lose faith and trust in yourself coz it will only cause you
to accomplish all that you could (can).

Jhanvi

Spirituality- It's Mystical

I think it's the beginning of the end,
While in reality I am being prepared for
The worst, whilst making me strong
And it's all being done by the supreme
Power, by God

As I lay in the bed, thinking about the
Things unsaid,
About those events which happened even
When I lost all hope
And now I understand, for that was
Possible solely because of the fact that I
Trust Him;

I have surrendered myself to Him,
I have given away all doubts of mine,
Trusting His ingenious methods of
Showing me the path I need to choose.

The path He makes me walk on, is not straight,
It's never straight;
But that shouldn't deny the fact that it
Is right and is the only way I can
Overcome the situation.

Begin this journey of finding yourself
And, knowing that there is this power
Behind every single occurrence.
And that He is there to heal you, to love
You and to teach you,
Taking you to a higher level of Consciousness.

And if I could say anything to Him, it would be,
"You are my strength when I am weak,
You are the treasure that I seek,
Seeking you as a precious jewel-
Lord to give up I'd be a fool.
When I fall, you pick me up
When I'm dry you fill my cup"

Spirituality- a word that got me
Thinking what It is,
Who is it that is greater than me, than you,
Yet is the most gentle, divine feeling
It leaves my body, mind and soul in a
Mystical condition,
Having control on every emotion of mine.

"Serve the lord with gladness, come
Before his presence with singing"

JK Bhagwat

Admiral Pereira: Episode I

As narrated by late Prof. TN Raina, ex-HoD, English department: Admiral Pereira, ex-Deputy Commandant of National Defence Academy was a very honest and conscientious officer. He never used government transport for personal use. His usage of government car started after he came to office. His lady wife used to drop him in their private car every morning and would pick him up after he finished work.

One morning, as he was alighting from their car, the Admiral spotted a cadet sneaking away from Sudan block with the obvious intention of bunking class. The Deputy Commandant shouted at him and called him, but the cadet sprinted. Admiral Pereira also sprinted to catch him, but the cadet vanished. After two rounds of Salaria Suare, he came back disappointed and furious and bidding goodbye to Mrs. Pereira, he climbed the steps of Sudan.

In the afternoon as they were having lunch Mrs Pereira casually asked him, if he could catch the cadet. "No!" replied the Admiral, "The .... was too fast for me."

"But dear, if you had troubled yourself to look at the shadowy bushes in the garden, you would have caught him. He was hiding in the shade till you went inside," said Mrs. Pereira.

"Why didn't you tell me," asked the angry Admiral.

"Well, it was between you and the cadet. Why should I have interfered in a fair competition?" said Mrs. Pereira.

The Admiral merely smiled and shrugged his shoulders and the matter ended there.

Admiral Pereira: Episode II

A true story of Admiral Pereira, ex-Deputy Commandant of National Defence Academy as narrated by late Prof. TN Raina, ex-HoD, English department.

Admiral Ronnie Pereira was the Deputy Commandant of the academy in the 70s. He was known for his very strict control over his jurisdiction and had a soft corner for junior cadets. In those days, junior cadets were often deprived of their issued items by seniors and were given old items to wear. During one inter-squadron athletic championship in Bombay Stadium, Admiral Pereira was watching the proceedings when a first termer passed by. He was wearing tattered socks which was noticed by the Admiral. "Come here!" shouted admiral Pereira and the cadet, frightened to the core came sprinting to him, "Do you know my residence?" asked the Admiral.

The poor cadet blurted, "Yes sir!", "Go to my house and report to Mrs. Pereira," ordered the Admiral. The cadet sprinted and went to the cycle stand to pick up his bicycle. Enroute, he managed to get the location of the Dy Commandant's house. When he reached the destination, he hesitantly rang the bell. Mrs. Pereira opened the door and asked the cadet, "Yes dear, what is it?" The cadet mumbled, "Ma'am, Sir has asked me to come to you."

"Okay, let me have a look at you," she said and scrutinized the cadet's outfit. Noticing the torn socks, she went inside and came back with a pair of new white socks. "Here you are dear," she said. "Wear those and report to your Deputy Commandant."

The cadet changed his socks replacing the torn ones with the new ones. After 20 minutes, he came back to Bombay Stadium and stood in savdhan (attention) in front of Admiral Pereira. "Now that is how you should be dressed," thundered the Admiral. "Carry on!" he ordered, and the cadet gleefully sprinted to his place in the stadium. Such was the strict yet soft hearted gentleman Admiral Pereira.

Jyotirmoy Ghosal
Monsoon! Love And Fury

Amidst the monsoon's tumultuous air,
An arena where hope meets despair,
A dance of melancholy and romance,
Two sides of a coin, in a cosmic trance.

Even as the clouds gather and storms brew,
Love and deceit are part of Monsoon's crew,
With torrents comes a deluge as rivers overflow,
Slush of landslides bring forth a tale of woe.

Floods cascade with fury and relentless might,
In this tempestuous love's flickering twilight;
The dichotomy of the season's joy and thrill,
In a kaleidoscope of emotions, love stands still.

In the moist lips of the Monsoon's embrace,
The love-birds sing with amazing grace,
As she yearns for her lover's song of love,
The sky opens as raindrops fall from above.

She awaits with bated breath, to be drenched,
In a rhythmic downpour their hearts entrench.
She dreams of him adorned in rain's delight,
But her wet lips quiver in an unknown fright;

In monsoon's symphony, hearts re-ignite,
Pure love gives out sparks ever so bright
Together, they find love, in rain and thunder,
In Monsoon's caress, love blooms down under.

The chiffon awaits, with whispered sighs,
To meet her skin to skin, where passion lies;
That tender touch, the last drop must win,
Love's journey goes deep, for life to begin.

Today's Wordsworth

I wandered lonely in the crowd....
Looking for flowers called 'daffodils'
Held by my neck, no escape allowed
I was hurled in the van that stood still!

Why was I in the crowd they asked me?
Why did I wander? I was taken in custody!
When Section 144 is imposed in town!
"You don't look for daffodils! You Clown!"

I was the unlucky star to shine,
My back bruised; I couldn't whine;
For I wanted to look for the daffodils
To have pleasure, that my heart fills.

Around the neck of the political boss,
To my delight I saw flowers flung across,
I saw the ghost of the golden daffodils;
When the van with yellow marigold fills!

Behind the bowers looking for the bliss
Lovers engaged in a delightful kiss!
Was it my imagination that got me caught
Or was it again, the Anti Romeo squad?

When the signal from red went green,

I felt the fluttering of violent breeze;
The cars honked and bikes vroomed
Looking for daffodils I was doomed!

I crossed the red signal, was dis-allowed,
As my mind floated like a cirrus cloud;
I was booked for too much Attitude!
When I said, "It was the bliss of Solitude!"

I got a baton upon my inward eye,
To my Solitude I finally bid good bye,
Never again would I be of any worth,
For Daffodils are only for Wordsworth.

Ketaki Pimplekhare
Memoir Of A Lucky Girl

Growing up as a child in the army is definitely a unique existence. While we changed schools all the time, roughly once in two years, we never wasted any time to make new friends wherever we would get posted.

As my father was in the armoured corps, our postings were mainly in large cantonments, away from the city or town. We would have to go to school either on our bicycle or in a three-ton truck (certified school bus for all the children going to schools) one of the most unique things to begin with.

There were always orderlies (*sahayak*) to help us, but they were primarily meant for the officer and if they did anything for us it from the goodness of their word and was not something we could demand. In any such case we would be reprimanded heavily by my father for misconduct. That was the first lesson to respect every human being no matter their rank or stature in society. And I'm ever so grateful for that.

The army is the epitome of secularity (not in the modern sense of the word) but truly meant that every culture or religion should be respected, and people should have the freedom to practice their faith no matter where they went.

Because of this, we celebrated every festival in the regiment or brigade and particularly looked forward to Holi as we could get a bit rowdy without any dire consequences.

When my father was posted in Ahmednagar, he was commanding the Auto regiment and I was studying college in Pune. I had taken my friends over there for my 16th birthday, and it was so special. We had the opportunity to ride on tanks in the range areas and the soldiers (bhaiyas, as we called them with affection) were so lenient with us, they let us do what we wanted, including driving the tanks one by one. I think it was nothing much for me but for my friends from the civil life it was the most memorable event of their life!!

They can't stop raving about their tank driving experience, even now which is almost 30 years later. It's the most unique things one can do. Also, we got to ride horses, motorcycles, swim, fire guns and take the cross-country trail wherever we wanted. Being three sisters, we never missed anything that a boy would normally do. And I thank my parents for never making the distinction and brought us up as any boy.

I hope you enjoyed reading this small memoir of a very lucky girl who has the fortune of being born to and Indian army officer.

Krishna Kumar

Mixture, The Panacea

Mixture is a heterogeneous combination of many elements. For the Keralites, mixture is the right combination of many edible components including the Curry Leaf and is a favoured accompaniment with alcohol. But, for the Cadets of Sainik School, Kazhakootam, the MIXTURE meant a light brown solution filled to brim in a big glass jar and administered to the unfortunate ones struck by fever....

Medical fitness was of utmost importance to us Cadets who were aspiring to be Soldiers of the future. The pre-selection medicals ensured that we were all structurally sound. An annual medical examination was also a part of the routine. The inoculation jabs, part of this annual ritual was a dreaded event. Examining of family jewels, for reasons unknown then, also embarrassed many of us.

Our doctor was a retired medico from Govt service. An elderly person, he remained unapproachable to the Cadets who sought asylum at the MI room for reasons ranging from genuine illness to feigning sick, to skip PT and examinations, as an extreme step. The pretenders had perfected the art so well, with the right expression of combined pain and weakness that many a times they got a better deal than the genuine ones. The most common ailment was a fever and like any other of our age group, we were also susceptible to this common viral infection. With a heavy head and blocked nose, one would get past the Prefect to 'report sick', a term found only in military lexicon.

With the sick report, book one would land up at the MI room, to be registered with the bulky Sick Register. An uneasy calm prevailed as one awaited his turn outside the Doctor's chamber. On stepping in, the Doctor, with the ability of an astute face reader would start scribbling beginning with Rx on his pad.

Before one could rattle out all symptoms, some genuine and some made up to add special effect, the Doc would have completed the prescription which started with the diagnosis, Coryza, something we tried hard to decipher those days. With few more symptoms yet to be disclosed, the sick is then forced to retract from the Doc's chamber as he calls out 'Next'.

The sick then marches to the medicine counter, where an Army Veteran, a compounder by qualification but considered better than a doctor by practice owing to his vast experience in handling the wounded in extreme field conditions, awaited the patient. The medicines for the 'out of the box' ailments would be given first and then the sick with fever would be lined up. At the counter was a big glass jar filled with a brown solution, the MIXTURE. A tablet given is to be shoved into the throat followed by a goblet filled to brim with the MIXTURE.

This panacea sort of concoction was the most dreaded of all. It had a combined taste of all unpalatable elements in the world and tasted so objectionable that the oesophagus would reject it with same vigour as it was pushed down. If the act of rejection occurred in front of the Compounder, one would be re-attached to the queue and administered the mixture again, while the sweeper would be tasked to clean up the mess. The mixture remained in the stomach for long with a "To throw up or not to" kind of feeling. Those who were declared SIQ, Sick in Quarters, hurried back to their dens and spent the day missing only their mother's care, something one longed for during such downtimes. Those given M&D, Medicine and Duty, would struggle with the classes bearing the discomfort of the MIXTURE inside their guts.

In later years, those of us who donned the uniform had sighted this deadly decoction at the MI Rooms in some of the training academies, qualifying it to be a 'Pan India Military Phenomenon'. How effective the mixture was in combating the pathogens was not certain, but the helpless cadets recovered fast and remained fighting fit, merely to be spared of the unpleasant encounter with the deadly MIXTURE....

Kumud Mishra

Excerpt From A Conversation With Pragya Bajpai

An introvert and shy by nature, actor Kumud Mishra is best known for his incredible roles in films like Thappad, Badlapur, Airlift, Jolly LLB 2, to name a few. He talks about his unconventional journey of discovering his love for theatre amidst the military school environment and how as a cadet, the military values shaped his character to face ensuing challenges in the pursuit of his career in cinema.

1. The Father Factor- Becoming an actor from a Military family and life

When my father was in the army, I saw him acting in a play titled 'Prithviraj ki Aankhein' which inspired me a lot. He was not only a good actor but also a good singer. He used to perform in Ramleela before getting into the army. Even my grandfather was a good singer. I think I have inherited acting skills somehow from my family. I was basically a quite a shy person; it is through theatre, I eventually started expressing myself.

2. Role of Military school in shaping the character and defining career

I studied in Military school, Belgaum for seven long years. It is there that my interest in theatre started taking shape. Discipline in the school articulated my objective of becoming an actor and encouraged me to focus on my goal. The school focused on the all-round development of every cadet. At the age of ten, we got a chance to come on to the stage and perform regularly. It was mandatory for every class to perform a skit once in a month. My teachers, Ne Pathade, Mr. Tapan and Mr. Janarthan encouraged me a lot. Once, I even shaved my head to perform in a skit; that was the kind of zeal inculcated in us by the school. Not so late, I watched Nasir saab's film 'Paar' in the school when I decided to join theatre and make it my profession.

3. The Bhopal Angle

After passing out from the school, I came to Bhopal to stay with my parents. As I didn't have friends over there, my father enrolled me in a theatre workshop organised by Shri Alakhnandan ji. I used to walk for five kilometres every day to attend the workshop and I always used to be punctual which impressed the director of the workshop. This element of self-discipline and persistence, I inherited from the Military school, Belgaum.

4. Challenges

I always used to think that I would join the army and continue theatre there also. Even in my SSB interview, my prime focus was on the theatre only. Nevertheless, if you take it seriously, theatre is an exhaustive area that demands an extensive study, but only close to perfection. Professional challenges and struggles are still on and seems to be never ending. I traveled a lot to Bombay from Bhopal in search of work. I borrowed a sum of Rs. 3000 (not a small amount in 1990s) from my school friend to begin my new journey. Till date, I haven't returned that money, because it was not just Rs. 3000 but something akin to a lucky charm that changed my life forever.

I haven't struggled much as I got work in the initial stage of my stay in Bombay. But the ultimate struggle was to prove myself and maintain consistency.

5. The Roles I like!!

Before choosing my role in a film, I am more interested in looking at the script and the screen play. I decide to accept my role based on that, irrespective of its length or importance in the film. I like many roles I have done, but I never identify myself with any of them. Most of the times, the character we think is easier to play happened to be extremely difficult to perform. I personally find Anubhav Sinha's character in the movies like Thappad, Article 15 and Mulk extremely challenging to perform.

6. Armed Forces and Cinema

Initially, whenever I met my school friends who joined the armed forces, I missed being in 'the uniform'. Now, after coming to the world of cinema, those regrets are not there as I get chance to wear a uniform and perform. I feel elated to get invited by my fauji friends to stage theatre in their respective units.

Cinema/ theatre relieves stress from people's day to day busy life in the armed forces, people are always on the move and busy with their work schedule. Cinema offers them a great relief. This was well proved during the COVID-19 period. For that matter, the world relied upon entertainment industry during those tough days. Many faujis now-a-days are sending their children into the entertainment industry. It is gaining momentum due to the introduction of OTT platforms.

7. Who am I

I am a simple and ordinary man doing my job with honesty. I don't think that mine is a great profession which is unique and outstanding. Rather, I believe every work/ profession is special and everyone is doing their job; be it a doctor, teacher, engineer, fauji or sweeper. It all depends on how each one takes it; what makes the difference is how they perform. Everyone has different kinds of struggles, only they can understand what they go through.

8. Balancing personal and professional life

My nature of job is such that, if we have work, we are busy for months together. And when we are free, we are at leisure. Since my spouse is also an actress and from the family of theatre, we understand each other better. Keeping the needs of our son in mind, we balance our work schedule. Now, he is grown up and we don't have such problems. Having a spouse from your own field of work helps us understand our professional commitments well, especially in the film industry. During my free time, I prefer to stay at home and read books and at times connect with my Military school friends and relive those days that remain close to my heart.

Lily Swarn

Excerpt From The Gypsy Trail: Travels And Travails Of An Army Wife

Wedded life began in earnest, in the sylvan surroundings of the picturesque hill town Dalhousie. It was built in 1854 by the British Empire as a summer retreat for its troops and officials. Built across five hills it is dotted with Scottish and Victorian architecture. Beautiful churches and bungalows lend it a quaint old-world charm. The revered poet Rabindranath Tagore visited Dalhousie, in 1873, and Rudyard Kipling came, in 1884. The gigantic snow laden Dhauladhar peaks stand guard like sentinels.

We gathered straw and twigs for our minuscule nest in the pint-sized cantonment, called Baloon Cantonment. British troops moved here, in 1868. It was originally created to be a convalescent spot due to its salubrious climate. Prime Minister Jawaharlal Nehru visited, in 1954, for the centenary celebrations of Dalhousie.

I can never forget my first home after marriage as it was loaded with numerous historic 'firsts' in my life. It was a ground floor house made primarily of wood and was the official accommodation for Captains. We heard that in the British era Sergeants of the army lived here. Families of troops deployed on the Afghanistan and Baluchistan borders were housed here. The house was furnished with basic furniture but to my naive young mind it was my castle and queenly domain. I used to rush home from work from the Sacred Heart College that used to be under the diocese of Lahore. Many nuns from Lahore had to stay back in this convent during partition. It is a majestic building where many film shootings took place. Films like 1942, A Love Story and Gadar were shot here. An army vehicle called a three tonne, bulky though sturdy transported me up the steep hill to work. My husband's office was a hop and a skip away from home, so he merely trudged through the snow in winters. The homes had cheerful fireplaces where we lit log fires in the evenings. The crackle of a wood fire still makes my heart skip a beat and makes me want to hum a song. I remember carrying home wild daisies that grew profusely on the lush hill slopes.

Wordsworth's daffodils grew in a carpet full of yellow bunches nodding their fragrant heads. It was like a vacation home for me. I would fill the house with jugs full of blooms. As there were very few vases in my worldly possessions, I simply arranged flowers in any available glass or dish.

My memory pulls me to the utterly adorable trailing vines of rambler roses clinging to the slopes near Charing Cross. I pulled out a few creepers regularly to add greenery inside my little sitting room. The afternoons were filled with a leisurely game of croquet on the lawns. Hitting wooden balls through square topped hoops with wooden mallets was a lot of fun. Much cheer and bonhomie prevailed over the game in which all officers and their wives participated.

There was an intriguing phenomenon, which was truly spooky in our first ever home. Well as we rose each morning and sleepwalked into the washroom, we would find the soap missing? We could not for the life of us find a suitable or likely excuse to explain this daily occurrence. Each morning we replaced the bar of soap until one day the lady who lived in the house above ours met us and said, "Do you know we have a new bar of soap in our bedroom every morning!" Imagine our bewildered mirth mingled with horror when we realised that this was the handiwork of the rather well fed and scary looking rats that lived in the rafters of our ceiling. These rats scurried up the chimney of the fireplace with our belongings, safely depositing them in the house above. Once they even stole some roses made of wax from a wall hanging and whisked them away.

The memorable moments of this almost extended honeymoon posting for us were the treks and picnics to the Kalatop – Khajjiar sanctuary. Thickly forested by deodar trees the Kalatop rest house is ensconced in lonesome grandeur. Kalatop is also a paradise for bird watchers. One can spy the Eurasian Jay, white winged black bird, black headed Jay, chestnut bellied Rock Thrush, Grey Headed Canary Flycatcher. Khajjiar has a curious floating island on a small stream fed lake and the famous ancient Khajji nag (serpent god) temple. It was built by the Pandavas in 12th century AD to worship the nag devta. The snake God is believed to reside in the Khajjiar Lake. This unique bowl of green meadows is known as the Switzerland of the East.

A walk around the cool road in Dalhousie is unforgettable for its breath-taking views. The aroma of luscious Bharmour apples tingles the nostrils. The serenity of this hill cantonment calls out to me for a revisit. It will always remain special for me as my daughter was born here in a little dispensary.

Monisha Rastogi

Resilience Of A Fauji Wife

I have it in me
A kind of resilience that I am proud of
I have it in me
To get up and bounce back when life turns rough
and one gets engulfed in storms

I cannot let the waves of defeat
Overtake and drown me
I bounce when I see and feel the rainbows
In the midst of a storm
And I quickly adapt and learn to glide through it
Just like a new-born
Isn't this resilience that surfaces in me
And makes me strong

Running errands from dusk to dawn
Donning the role of a dad and a mom
With bright robe of a smile on
That's me... a fauji wife!
With resilience by my side
I take the world in my stride

I have families to look after
And take to their untimely calls

When my man does his duty at far off seas
And leaves me with responsibilities
I, with pride, take every stride
Only a few resilient wives can tide

Most give up and many cry
It's a tough life .... when your man is away
Most of the times
But for me, Duty Honour Courage
Comes First... Each and Every time
Whether it was the birth of our son or our silver anniversary
Or even my milestone birthday

My man with Honour by his side
Has always sailed, protecting the oceans
And I.. like a true fauji wife
Have celebrated these occasions
Knowing well, that Nation needs him more
Than me or my time!

In And Out Of Boxes

My married life as a defence officer's wife
Started with a couple of unique boxes
Aluminium, wooden, cardboard to name a few!

And stored in them are now memories
That pop up like a jinn
Fulfilling the wish of a time machine
Which transports me to time serene

Oh! those days of boxes
Where are thou gone?
Leaving behind beautiful memories
That still have the power to bond

Boxes that turned into a bed
Where I fell into the world of dreams
And the same took over as a settee
When guests came umpteen

Some used as table tops, some as storage bins
And some with a lock and key
To house the jewels of a fauji wife
In its safe precincts
The rank and name of my husband
Hand Painted on each box
With a sense of elan and pride

That only can be understood by the warrior tribe

We even numbered our boxes
That spoke of our organisational skill
And inside was put a label
Of the lovely stuff kept within

One full of silk sarees
Another full of kitchen frills
That immediately grounded you
And balanced all the thrill

Curtains, bedsheets and show pieces
When unpacked from the box
Adorned the walls of a govt house
And created some Class!

The out of the box thinking of a fauji wife
Can definitely be credited
To living out of boxes most of her life

In today's world of packers and movers
Who have made our transfers a bliss
I still miss those days of boxes
Which could house a Home within

Nandita De Nee Chatterjee
Silent Saviours

Unborn nation, a foetus
Magnificent men undergoing rigorous training.
15,200 km land frontier
Coastline 7516.6 km
To man a country formed in 1500 BCE
A handful of noble men in 1932
Metamorphosed to 170,576 actives in 2017, reserve 140,000
Third most powerful Air Force globally
Fourth in the world military hierarchy

Officers and gentlemen of the Indian Military
In the spotlight for reclaiming their land...
Lifelong dedication to service before self

Ninety years old Indian Vayu Sena
'Nabhaḥ Spr̥śaṁ Dīptam'
'Touch the Sky with Glory'
The Indian Eagles soared.
Magnificent men with their flying machines
Securing airspace for 1.417 billion citizens

Critical for the Indian firmament
Army, Navy and Air Force, Coast Guard
Suffering immeasurable casualties
Sans leave, families, facilities,

Tough terrains, tougher calls
Saving a brand-new nation
From interminable assaults
Wars, terror attacks, border skirmishes
Rescue operations in worldwide disasters
Manmade and natural

Every evil offensive handled fearlessly.
Young marshals of our land
The National Anthem their beacon call
The Indian Defence Force
A force the world reckons with
Trained and relentless in their defence
Disciplined and dedicated in their missions
Even when impossible
Noble in their commitment
Dangerous and deadly on aggression

Forgotten by their citizens
Unaware of the extremities faced

A nation living peacefully
Sleeping safely

The military works on silently
A carefree world their ultimate reward.

Navdeep Multani

Emotions In Olive Greens

Emotions in context of a soldier play a larger-than-life role for this always morally upright and polished man. This battle-hardened fellow is often exposed to risks where a simple twist of fate, can make him a hero or send him to his grave. He has, in a remarkable contrast, a fragile corner deep within the otherwise stone hard heart. The unique wheel of life, which begins with an early departure from home at an age, when most of us are referred as adolescents, to these makeshift homes called barracks; it comes a full circle the day he hangs his boots. During these intervening years, spent with his comrades who come from every walk of life, a soldier also finds himself draped in emotions on various occasions.

A career in the armed forces is starkly marked with various moves from one city to another at regular intervals. Every place of posting brings in new friends, new companions, and even strange bedfellows, who leave an indelible print on his psyche. In this remarkable career, where camaraderie, brotherhood, love, and respect for each other are the basis of foundation for friendship, the threads of which grow stronger with every passing moment, a buddy acquires the status of an icon. He is a prized possession of every soldier, in whom he can confide his deepest personal thoughts, feelings of fun and sorrow. Then it is time to move again. Farewell notes are exchanged, and the moist eyes convey what the choked throat cannot.

Though the new station of posting will again bring new acquaintances, but the memories of the last posting linger for a long time. Postings to field areas at frequent intervals lead to long and protracted separations from family and friends. During leave, every soldier eagerly looks forward to spending some valuable time with his near and dear ones. He is enthusiastic, brimming with joy and charged with ebullience while proceeding from his adopted home on leave. But this very arrival at 'own home' is always followed by departure, which again entails separation, thus touching the very soft corner in his heart, making him highly emotional. It makes him pensive, disconcerted with the thought that now memories would soon only be what he will live with till he meets them again.

Then sometimes Cupid strikes the bachelors, and it is time to tie the nuptial knot. And if some enterprising fellow has gone to great lengths to win the hand of his beloved, the matters get worse at the time of joining the duty. The pangs of his first separation coupled with the rhetoric of newly wed bride (to get leave extended) cause his mental faculties to blink. Finally giving her a false pretence that he would be back soon, he returns to the barracks with a heavy heart. He remains aloof for a few days, seldom talking to his buddies about his marriage and separation, long before he returns to his usual self.

Letters from home ringing news of near and dear ones evoke a mixed response amongst the soldiers, depending upon whose letter it is. Everyone awaits the arrival of 'dak' with deep set eyes which exudes confidence but hides the fear deep seated in his heart as to what news it would bring. Nevertheless, it is the facial expression after the dak has been disbursed which reflects, in sharp contrast, the jubilation at receiving two or more letters and the mournful and crestfallen appearance of those having received none. With letters in hand, everyone tries to find that secluded corner, where he can read it over and over again till his fertile imagination takes a flight of fancy beginning to daydream about times spent with his family and friends. This flight is abruptly sabotaged by the whistle of Battery Havildar Major, for its time to resume work again. Those unlucky to receive any letter, quietly take out an old one to read and, if caught kissing it unawares, would give a sheepish look saying, "just received it today only", though the month-old date clearly belies his claim.

Amongst all the difficult times and the storms in the challenging and tough life of a soldier, one that hits him the hardest, is the loss of his comrade. This loss brings forth excruciating painful emotions. He is abruptly stripped of any illusions about his own immortality. No longer might he comfort himself with the thought that his buddy was in line ahead of him. He feels newly alone and vulnerable and, more than ever, responsible for his life. With this loss, a rite of passage seems to have taken place in a second, leaving him on his own, without his assistance.

The word 'alone' stays with him. It spins in his head and lugs at his feelings. It destroys anything that is remotely pleasant. In that time of feebleness, he feels knocked down, but struggles to find his moorings again because it was part of life and not an end. At the memorial service, he salutes the martyr in silence with moist eyes as he files past the tombstone on which the inscription would read-

"Brother when you weep for me,

remember it was meant to be

As you lay me down in grief,

I shall always be at your sleeve.

Brave hearted and born to die,

because we chose

Duty before life"

Navneet Grewal

Let Love Hold

Scattered lie the dictums
Some braise, some freeze
Heartless syntax inked
Drilling nails in each walking coffin

Festooned will every dawn wakes
Holding the board for darts ready
Oozing tears cocktailed in blood
Concoctions as therapy in our rucksacks

Enroute gazing optimists
Acceptance embossed all over
Encrypted to dish warmth
A gooey whirlpool waits

Shocks you to life
Soul soups garnished
Soup sticks of embrace
Susurrations solicited please

The greatest incalescence
Love holds
Guillotine critique

Let each heart grow
Alive is what we must be
Enamoured to friendships
Enamoured to living
Diamante tears dry from each brow
A heartbeat precious we all hold
Let's love without being told

Proud Indians

In directions unlimited
We complete the birth, the journey, the process
Resilient yet bonding
Skyscrapers or highway jams

The skin shades vary
Of mahogany, browns even deep chocolate
A subtle pristine fairness
As the wood our incense and essence

Turbans, robes, nine yards
Elegance so varied yet rich
Couture gets the world to our doorstep
Radiates in our shadows twitch

Vermillion shades married to the turmeric
Cardamom flows in our blood
The love of our *Tiranga* is our pride
The *Chakra* taking us places on its ride

Deep friendships shower
As mirrors we reflect in taste
Miles away yet shouldering each girth
This congruence depicts our birth
Ingredients tossed with love
Accede the taste buds

Brewing the affair

As the menu differs in every strands cusp

We carry yarns of our culture

Follow and encircle with affection each brand

The world is just incomplete without Indians

We find them in every land

Sacrificing for their motherland

Some return wrapped in its flag

Let the world be aware

Bharatiya is our forever tag

Paromita Mukherjee Ojha

A Sneak Peek Into The Heart Of A Submariner's Wife: Past To Present

You are not defined by your past. You are prepared by your past.- Unknown

Well, today after 15 years of marriage that had its ample share of turbulence and calm, I decided to take a furtive look at the times spent with my submariner, some very memorable and some catastrophic, yet each day a learning experience and a mélange of precious memories.

Flashback: a girl with dreams to fly and live life 'queen size' working with a reputed airline interacts with a handsome young man on a popular social networking site mistaking him for a past batch mate. God in his heaven contrived to set the ball rolling and that casual acquaintance changed to something deeper.

After much conundrum once she joined her submariner in Visakhapatnam, she was immediately dropped in a flat in Naval Park and her gallant knight went off sailing squashing her dreams of setting up home together. The very same night the wife was greeted by a bat since there was no window frame installed in one of the bedrooms and later by a rat scampering away in full glory within the house. Imagine her plight, to view at such close quarters such unwelcome guests with no hope of rescue as the flat opposite and immediately below were vacant, nor any superhero like 'Spiderman' dropped by. The wife with trepidation decided to let the visitors continue their nocturnal mission solely in the bedroom by locking it from outside and slept in the hall reciting the lines which seemed to mock at her plight now *'God is in his heaven, and all is well with the world'*. Well, God definitely was in heaven, but all was surely not well in her world at least.

The doorbell rang one fine morning, with the wife in for a rude shock, when she opened the door to an unkempt, bearded stranger with a strange smell all over him. With some effort she recognized her 16-day old husband who no sooner walked inside the house, immediately walked out to much chagrin of the wife, who had spent hours trying to do-up the house making the best use of the limited resources available. She ran after her husband calling him back who returned dazedly refusing to believe this was the house, he had left her in fifteen days back.

The house eventually turned into a retreat of solace and comfort for the man and the wife i.e. me and my husband with the tapestry of our married life enriched by our friends from the naval fraternity, the ward-room get-togethers and constant witty reminders from the seniors and juniors alike in INS Sindhuraj, INS Sindhurakshak, INS Vagli that my husband is a *'one of his kind'* in the arm (no submariner remotely thinks of marriage in dolphin training time) as he did in true 'filmi' style charging in to 'secure' me (and his life), when the 'ballast tank' of our love life was overflowing with my tears due to ASW(anti-submarine warfare) strategy of the parents.

After 15 eventful years, I've learnt to cope with the unannounced late-night calls from bachelors demanding coffee and snacks, the creepy and crawly visitors abounding in NOFRA, the familiar strange smell (of diesel, oil, grime, grease and passion) my husband carries home when he returns from his sailings, I have mastered the acrobatic skills required to climb down the greasy ladders of the boat. I cherish the salutes given by men in uniform while I am in the gangway (has an old-world charm of its own). Today, I feel proud to share my bildungsroman with all, as it is in Naval bases that I learnt to cherish the bounty that life has offered me and God willing, I am not willing to let go off it anytime soon.

Rainbow Of Hope

The prismatic arch
Stretching from heaven to earth
Makes my hope surge
You are the calm after the storm
You give joy to soul's forlorn
Are you the pathway to angels' descent?
Connecting the dots between past and present.
Each of your hues distinct
Each boundary succinct
Blurring the precincts
Like the Crescent moon
You are a boon
To mankind petrified
Of impending annihilation
Due myopic devotion
To weapons of mass destruction
You are the harbinger
Of God's benediction
As long as man doesn't
Loose his eye for appreciation
Of God's beauteous creation
There will always be rainbow of hope.

Bonds Of Faith

My soul is indebted to this bond of faith
That has cradled my spirit
Plucking tirelessly my anxiety
Everyday brought new sights, new hopes
I learnt to embrace new vistas
Life need not be spent walking on tightrope
New day, rang in new possibility
Rejuvenating long buried abilities
Change is inevitable
What initially seemed insurmountable-
Has become a way of life inevitable
Every posting brought new friends, new hopes
I rose above the encircling doubts
Holding hands of new found bonds
My heart bursts from the seams
With treasure trove of precious memories
Every step of the way
I was blessed with strangers who became friends in need
Who lived by decree of sisterhood effortlessly
Time never mattered
Night or day, these friendships strengthened
My self-belief
Made life worth living
Living within the cherished walls of NOFRA
Has empowered me to find true strength within
Nothing ruffles my flights of faith

As I know my bevy of well-wishers
Are there with to keep me away from despair.
Life within the protected walls seems tough
When my man-in- white goes battling with seas rough
The friends within this blessed naval community
Are always there protecting me from doubts
They have never left me alone midway
Wordlessly, walking with me night and day.
Every day I wake up thanking God
For this blessed life that he has conferred.

Pragya Bajpai

Soldier's Memory

They march in squads with heavy backpacks
in camouflage rig
Pace steady without batting an eyelid
The semblance of anxiety and exhaustion is different
emerging from raging currents
Resilience can't be measured in rise and fall of mercury
that turns into a picture-perfect memory

Shoulders strong, made of steel
getting chiselled to strike at the call of duty
in the heart of darkness
Carry bags stuffed with some metallic fate,
old stories from course mates,
some miracles from the battlefield,
to feed the hungry heart with prerequisite zeal

Somewhere a mother cooks his favourite meal
she waits for him to join the festivity
And he eats survival food in solitude
somewhere close to the barbed wires
hundred miles away from the worldly ties
and endless desires
The food tastes well in solidarity
Peppered with joys and pains shared with men

of equal temper and equal mind
And after two decades down the line
they call it best of all times
The echoing sound of bombs, bullets, bloodshed
The hidden strategies, stories, secrets
The silent wonders buried in chest
The memory of war and piercing war cries
end only with life
not with time

Murder Of A Braveheart

A soldier returns home in Kashmir
dreaming of morning glories, *kebabs*, curries
and no worries

Militants like wild wolves prowling in the bush
barge into the discreet wedding to ruin his dream
No one knew what the family reunion
had in store after a decade long compulsive separation
from a son serving the nation somewhere in the distant land

Heaved out of home, dragged through the stairs
like a newspaper plane, he was tossed in the market place
for daring to weaken the militant's movement
threatening the idea of freedom
Homecoming is not a place of eternal damnation
But the son of the soil, betrayed by his own
was penalized for harbouring nationalism

His choice was denied
Yet the dreams were meant to stay in his eyes

They were many, furious and ruthless
Alone but a warrior he was, ever fierce and fearless
eyes relentless

The militants rejected the aging parents' plea for mercy
In the crowd of cowards amidst the unrest
The young soldier was cast off like a bitter end of a cucumber
and with that one murder
every nation lover of the city was warned
at the time of conception

The conflict of interest costed a blooming lotus
Nothing breaks your heart the way reality does
The helpless heaven on earth
mourned his death with the nation
He once said as a newly joined cadet,

"Choosing the army is more difficult than dying for the country"
The brave Kashmiri boy's silent promise to change his fate
and defend the nation, I perceived of late

A soldier is neither a superhero nor a God
He is a real patriot !

(In the memory of my Kashmiri student, Shaheed Lt Ummer Fayaz, 129 NDA)

Pravin Raghuvanshi

Welcome Vikrant In New 'Avatar'..!

Your majestic presence spreads the fragrance,
Glittering surfaces exuberate the appearance!
Mighty Vikrant, you sure are implausibly salubrious,
Leaving the adversaries cowed, baffled and envious!!
With exuding aura, in every Avatar you've been sailing,
Piercing the fathomless seas, with celestial fury trailing!
With tireless perseverance, you've achieved countless goals,
Though always laden with multi-faceted daunting roles!!
Your aircrafts thunder like typhoons, be it day or night,
Dominate the limitless skies, with all your aerial might!
O Vikrant! Endless is the saga of your audacious glories,
Shall always have fond and indelible memories!!

Your memories, O' Vikrant, with rise and fall of tide,
Would always be sung with frisson and pride!
Wondrous joy that the zeitgeist has always extended,
Sure you'd motivate the generations, whenever needed!!

O, Indomitable Carrier, you sure had left a big void,
Irreparable loss to the Navy, leaving it grossly devoid!
But your mightier reincarnation has cheered the Nation
For you'll win innumerable battles, with your gumption!!

Night At The Hamlet Of Paragon

Exordium

Back home from the inexorable schedules of flying in the sweltering

heat of Arakkonam, a pleasant surprise was there to greet me like a cool

breeze from the snow-clad mountains to rejuvenate the fatigued mind, body

and soul. Yes, it was an invitation most aesthetically rolled into a silvery

paper with a golden thread, which read:

The Peregrination

The benedictories of pantheon of Rajali intercede your presence to transform the tranquillity of "Hamlet of Paragon" into a breath taking, blizzardy reverberations of zither. The exotic aroma of blissful sumptuous cuisine spanning across the culinary spectrum is there to tantalize your appetite. So, the lasting frisson of vivacious environ of festivity awaits your rendezvous at Officers' Mess.

Date: 05 Nov, Time: 2000 hrs onwards

Dress: Innovative

Impregnate with inexplicable excitement, ever confused me, decided to attire as a Pathan, with an authentic Pathani suit adorned with a proud turban on head. As I set course for my peregrination towards this Hamlet of Paragon, the very tempting thought of encountering the swashbuckling benedictories of pantheon of hamlet truly exhilarated me.

The Encounter

As I approached the outskirts of hamlet, the sound of ceaselessly flowing fountain like a mountainous river hurtling down, diminishing into soft murmurs and giggles of the angels. Sure enough the entrance to this par de excellence did resemble like the gateway to the Paradise. The resonance of zither pervading the environs, the air permeating the celestial fragrance while the dangling-dandelions and daphnes were truly enchanting. The pathway to sanctum sanctorum rolled with red carpet had sprightly dressed fairies, laden with breathtaking ornaments, lined up either side forming an arch. The mesmerizing spray of rose water and a downpour of velvety soft petals was like a touch of fluff in the Quaker's line. Inner Core of the Hamlet

The inner core of the Hamlet was buzzing with activities. All the menfolk were draped in myriad sprightly-hued fancy attires, —ranging from Adam to Sherlock Homes, Emperor Akbar to Chieftains of nomadic tribes, Cowboys from west to Sheiks from Gulf and scores of others. A sea of humanity swelled up there, in a buoyant mood, adorn with opulence and vivacity, in a high-decibel festive environment.

Décor

The décor of the hamlet was truly innovative, it looked like an oasis with brook. The lush green velvety grass carpeted the terrain, suffused with thickly wooded coconut trees wrapped up with colourful creepers that celestially exuberated the appearance. Scores of rainbow-hued lights gave an appearance of twinkling stars in an enigmatic sky, with an occasional peeping of moon through the thin veil of clouds.

Ambrosia

The intoxicating beverages and variety of sumptuous food items were in abundance which covered the culinary spectrum. The delicious cuisine encompassed the menus ranging from rustic village to continental, Mughlai to Chinese and some even unknown. And, what more! Personally served by the angels with a bewitching smile, made it taste like ambrosia.

The Celestial Dance - The activities encompassed the angelic dances, imaginative games and nail-biting competitions. The solo dance performed by one of the benedictories was truly exalting, full of life and sensuous, which cast a spell-binding effect on the guests. The personal interaction with one the nymph was enchantingly exhilarating, as we exchanged smiles, giggles and guffaws.

Epilogue

The wondrous zeal and opportunity that the zeitgeist extended shall always form an indelible memory of the night spent at the Hamlet of Paragon in a festive environ in the enchanting company of celestial nymphets. Having consumed excessive ambrosia, and intoxicated with nectary beverages I swaggered back in a delirious mood thinking of all the charming benedictories of the pantheon. Only to be woken up next morning with a familiar voice chiming in my ears: "Good morning, Mr. Pathan! Here's your hot cup of tea...!"

Priya Khanna

Army Blues: Where Living Apart Is A Way Of Life

Being an army child, it was but natural that I would marry into the army. In fact, when relatives suggested prospective matches for me, they focused on finding an army officer. Soon I was married and became an "army wife." But as my brand-new husband was braving the enemy and harsh weather conditions at Siachen glacier when we got married, it was a while before we could actually set up a home together. So, I never actually felt "married" for the first few years. I just moved from one set of parents to another. Once an officer called and asked to speak to Mrs Khanna, I told him to wait for just a minute, while I went hunting for the older Mrs Khanna, who was the only "Mrs" I knew…. Then I realized, I was now both a Khanna and a Mrs. I couldn't stop giggling for a while afterwards.

That became the leit motif of my married identity. I was married but was mostly on my own for many of the initial years of my marriage, while my husband moved from one non-family station to another. All the stuff I bought for my home stayed packed in trunks and boxes in one location or another, while I continued to live in a single bedroom, now in my parents' home. We would set up home in one city and within 2-3 years he would leave for the border, and I would be back to my parents' home. Neighbours would wonder if I was still married or divorced, as I was regularly living with my parents. Then my husband would arrive on leave, and they would realise that I was still married!

People would ask how I could live like this, then answer their own question, saying 'Oh, you must be used to this'. Finally, I started replying that I also get used to staying with my husband when he's posted to a family station or even when he comes on leave. We all get used to every state of being. But the change is always hard.

Life moved on and I kept adjusting to living with him and alternating with living without him. After a few years, we were blessed with a daughter. As all daughters do, she asserted her complete dominance on her father, and both are best friends and do most activities together. However, whenever he has to go away from us on temporary duty or on a non-family posting, she finds it very difficult to adjust to the separation. I observe myself at such times and realise how I have now truly become used to these separations. They don't affect me as they used to in the past. But once he returns, even though there may be no obvious difference to my daily routine, I find that I tend to sleep better with him in the house. His presence brings peace to my soul.

I find this applies to everyone in the house, including our pet dog who suffers terribly when his master is away. No matter how many treats I give him or how much I scratch his ears, the dog runs to wait at the front door for his master to return and I have to keep dragging him back to my room, as I know no one is coming for a while. So, it's not just the army wives who adjust to separations, it's also the army children and army pet dogs who experience the pangs of separation from their beloved family member, an army man!

After all, a home is incomplete without each member of the family. Yet, I wouldn't exchange the army way of life for any other. I accept it all, the good with the bad. I think that is the true lesson I have learnt in my life, to embrace change and accept it for what it is, instead of fretting for what is not or comparing my life with others, because I'm a proud army wife!

Previously published in the online journal Yours Positively on September 10, 2021.

Raj Krushna Mishra
My Weary Sigh

It'll need a lifetime for soft reminisces of my sigh to take effect!
Although I possess an impatient greed
I'll not live until your
lustrous tresses turn grey!
Where's gone your feelings?
Aren't you perturbed to see my limitless passion?
And desperate desire for your pursuit?
How to deal in interim, with my recalcitrant heart ?
When will you notice my beaming love?
Agreed, you won't leave
me like an unclaimed orphan, but see
Am I not destined to die?
By the time you ruefully realise my love, it would
be too late
As I'd be on pyre, burning, into ashes!
I wonder if there's anyone who may have a cure to
my profound sorrow?
Nevertheless, I pray,
For a candle to burn until
the next dawn!

Reena Singh

The Army Thrives On Communal Harmony

The army may be perceived as being elitist in a way, what with its unique tradition and lifestyle of setting its members apart from "mere" civilians. But beneath that veneer of exclusivity runs a strong sentiment of inclusivity, because typically in all army cantonments or residential localities, people of several religions and communities live together in brotherhood as one. There is no evidence of a North-South divide, nor are there cultural differences between Punjabi and Christian families or Muslims and Nepalese. What is apparent is the more than a perfunctory interest in each other's ceremonies and rituals, of going beyond mere social trappings and getting to know the real person behind their masks of religion and social groups.

I remember my mother who till she passed away recently at 91, routinely harped about our 'glorious' army heritage based on the many postings that my father had across the country. In one of them, she would recall sharing a mess kitchen with a Nepalese major's family; and of the two families eating Nepalese delicacies along with the Punjabi food the two families would cook. The Nepalese family, too, developed a firm taste for the *choley-puri* and *kaali daal* cooked with great affection by my mother.

In another place, we had a neighbour from the north-east; in yet another, I was dispatched every evening to learn Hindi from a jovial older collegian in the area – a Muslim from Jammu called Khalid. His father, whom we would address as Khan Uncle was in the Army's Education Wing. We children were always welcome in their home.

In my early years, my Mom and Dad were best friends with a Colonel David in Meerut and an interesting old bachelor called Major Thomas who lived his retired life in some kind of a refurbished railway coach. I still have photos of clinging on to the three daughters of Colonel David, the eldest of whom was Sweety, in several of my sixth birthday party pictures. And I have fond memories of evenings spent in their sprawling home in Meerut.

In Ahmedabad and Agra, where Dad was posted at different times, a three-ton truck, fitted with special benches would lumber along every morning, ferrying us to school from the Cantonment. No one knew who among us was Bengali or Sikh, Keralite or Maharashtrian – we were just a happy bunch of students, merrily singing along or playing word games as we drove the long distance from cantonment to school. We learned a fisherman's dance in school that we later performed with great aplomb in an Army Durga Puja function. If I recall right, there was only one Bengali called Krishna in the motley group that performed. But it was like dancing for our own, *Apne Log*.

My brother and I have stayed as PGs with retired Army families (friends of the family) when we began work – my brother with an Assamese family, and me, with a Punjabi family. The common denominator was the Army and the close friendship that my parents had struck up with these diverse families.

In Agra, we lived near the regimental mandir and early mornings, a song would play out on its loudspeaker:

Dekh tere sansar ki haalat kya ho gayi bhagwaan

kitna badal gaya insaan, kitna badal gaya insaan...

I would hum along, thinking nothing of the meaning behind the lyrics back then. It was just a catchy tune playing every morning. Forty-five years later, as I write this, I can't but shudder at how true the words ring out now. Did the mandir's *pujari* know where we were heading?

In the army, you change cities, schools, and houses, every couple of years. Change can be unsettling, but in the army, transition or relocation was never a problem, and a move to a new city, never intimidating. I remember in Delhi's Red Fort, where accommodation was scarce and the waiting list for family housing long, a young Hyderabadi officer and his pretty wife thought nothing of giving us their home as he trooped off for a few months for an army course in Pune. He locked up his personal belongings in the smallest room in the house and left the rest of the house in our charge. He came on leave, too, once; and the couple slept in the small, cramped room, happily eating with us! In the army, these are routine events – nobody thought it incongruous how a South Indian could lend his home to a Sikh family and then blend with near strangers in the same home while on a visit.

This is something the Army and PSUs like Indian Oil, NTPC and SAIL, Bokaro Steel City, Tata companies in Jamshedpur and the Navy and Air Force share; they acknowledge the cultural diversity of their employees, never segregating them. Every festival is celebrated, from Onam to Deepavali, Id and Christmas in a spirit of camaraderie and friendship. What I remember of these social evenings is not so much the rituals as the spirit, the fun and frolic.

What I also remember are neighbours you could count upon, of strangers turning up at your doorstep with a welcoming smile and hot flasks of tea, biscuits and sandwiches when you moved into a new home in a new cantonment, and of abiding warmth. When I compare this with my current, largely civilian neighbourhood where I have been living these past 21 years but have still not been able to penetrate the "clannish" camps of certain communities, I sigh. Had it been an army community, it would have transformed several dull evenings into vibrant social settings, where people would meet at the local community centre to play table tennis and badminton, as well as rounds of tambola on Sunday mornings or evenings.

Food, fun and games is the one formula that can bring people together, but alas, that is possible only when people are willing to let their hair down and accept people of all faiths just the way they are – without boundaries and conditions.

Previously published in the online journal, Yours Positively on August 24, 2021.

Renuka Shukla

Those Thrilling Days Of Yesteryears: A Memoir

There's a universal truth we have to face whether we want or not, everything eventually ends. But endings are inevitable. I have always disliked endings. Saying goodbye is the most difficult thing that school never teaches but those who believe in the concept of life don't agree to the whole idea of saying byes. It is just the end of one part but not the end of everything that is waiting beautifully in the next part of life.

I clearly recall the day when finally, the time had arrived to say goodbye to everything that we were familiar with, everything that we were so used to, all that had become the part and parcel of our lives. After serving for 36 years in the Indian Army as a medical officer with 'Army Medical Corps'. The time was drawing closer to hang his uniform 'Olive Green' and say goodbye and thanks to all those who supported us to sustain with pride. An occasion like this is a time for gratitude as well as reflection.

I always remained by his side as a lady wife for 27 years indulging myself with the values, ethos, traditions taught to me by other senior lady wives to maintain for the betterment of the organisation. Needless to say, that I have been extraordinarily lucky to get married to a medical officer who spent his entire precious years for the worthy cause to serve the nation as much as possible in the best of his capacities. The man in the 'olive green' as a healer and looking after the health of men, women and families with respect, admiration, care and lots of empathy.

I recall the year 1992 when we got married at Lucknow. The moment is making me nostalgic and compelling to go down the memory lanes of my past days. Varanasi was the station where I had joined him first as a newlywed. There I stayed for a year and blessed with a baby boy with the grace and blessings of Kashi Vishwanath. After a year we moved to a place called 'Chassad' situated on the borders of India-Myanmar. To reach the place itself was challenging. That was the time when north-eastern part of India was extensively disturbed with so many movements. It took 12 days to reach the place as the solo movement was restricted and was allowed only with the convoy. After crossing Bihar, Assam, Nagaland finally we reached our destination. I still have obvious memories of those difficult days.

It was a small village where the unit headquarter was located with minimal facilities excluding electricity, school, STDs, market the list is endless with a population of tribes like 'Naga' and 'Kuki'. The NSCN movement was in its full swing. It was entirely a new culture for me to experience right from the language to food. There was no accessibility to basic amenities like television, radio, newspaper and most importantly, fresh milk was not available. The survival was really challenging but exciting. I had an option to stay back at Lucknow but then I decided to avail the opportunity to stay together and surely it was the biggest motivation. It seemed as if I was away from the civilization. No source of any entertainment really made me discover myself in the lapse of natural beauty of the place.

I started writing diaries every day and read out my creativity to myself. I, myself was the listener as well as the reader. For one phone call I had to come down to 'Imphal' the capital of Manipur after traveling five hours by road with my small son. The movement of the officers were restricted because of the insurgency. I could speak to my parents once or twice in a year. The life was unimaginably challenging and tough with a small child.

With the help of the unit, we started a primary school with a single local teacher and five students. My son was one of them. But the best part was that we were together enjoyed best with the minimal facilities. We cherished the serenity of the natural beauty in the wildest form and the natives for their simple living and style. The modesty of this life taught us timeless lessons that helped us to remain happy, contended and grounded in the varied situations. After four years, we moved to Delhi followed by Jabalpur, Gangtok, Dehradun, Lucknow, Mhow, Pune and finally to Darjeeling, a place full of natural beauty.

30th of September was my husband's last day in the organisation. God has bestowed blessings on us, and we are now living our second inning with new hopes and dreams with dignity, poise, and grace against all odds! It's indeed the beginning of a new chapter in our lives but it is also a time to look back and reflect with pride on the achievements we have earned, a treasure chest of lessons learned in both good-hard times, we tried to stand tall against the test of times and situations and braved them all. In the new phase of life, we are trying to fulfil our dreams. Life is awaiting with new challenges every day for us but I'm sure, we would definitely champ them too with love and gratitude.

Roopali Sircar Gaur

Daddy's Uniform

I loved your olive green
uniform Dad.
Just touching it made my heart so glad.
I wanted to be like you.

I wanted to do the things you could
One day I believed I too would.

The brass stars on your shoulders
And the three lions
The lanyard with the whistle at the end
to be tucked into
Your left pocket.
Remember I never forgot to blow the whistle
every day before you left.

The polished boots its shine in every step of yours
So I would sit crossed legged on the floor
with the cherry blossom boot polish and
another one with an ostrich painted on
the slim black silver paper covered tin box.

The hard brush with which dad brushed
the sand and dust off your boots which
walked many miles in the hot desert sand.

The tin of brasso with its thick yellow liquid.
It was Mother who lovingly taught me how to
use the soft yellow cloth to rub the
stars and the three lions.

Sometimes I would pick up your Peak cap and
stand before the mirror and mother would
Say," never do that!
You have to earn it.
It's an honourable object
not for everybody to wear
You have to go through hell fire before the olive green you can
wear".
Since then, your cap dear dad
became a symbol of dare.

The special objects in our home
were strangers in other homes.
The "hussif" a small khaki coloured pouch
containing buttons, needles, and thread reels.

The fragrance of polish and brasso
The polishing tongs,
and the black trunk box
from which popped the blue patrols
The formal white Mess Dress
Which made you look so debonair.
I loved them all.

Lansdowne: "Home Of The Veer Garhwali"

Headless horse men, ghosts, tapping and the sound of horse hooves at midnight. Mysterious nocturnal happenings at night haunt cantonments. There are invariably a few old bungalows which dot the landscape are often known for being haunted. Mother had a tough time hiring help, thanks to these ghost sighting stories. We got used to living with them. English ghosts come knocking on moonless nights.

Graveyards in broken down church yards, some marked some unmarked let them out for a stroll. Ranz Potter, a professor who specialises in Gothic studies, says the headless horseman, as a supernatural entity, represents a past that never dies, but always haunts the living. "The headless horseman supposedly seeks revenge—and a head—which he thinks was unfairly taken from him," Potter says. Evenings in cantonments get eerie. The British an adventurous lot who came seeking their fortunes searched these wild cool hilly places. This is where they set up their army recruitment and training centres.

Everything happened in a precise military manner and much of it continues to date. They built bungalows and hired locals as bearers, cooks, and gardeners, saises and coolies. Thus, creating for themselves a *laat saheb's* life. The Burra Saheb was a revered persona. Unlike the memsahib who perforce had to deal with the house helpers. The constant fulfilling of the burra sahibs' requirements brought them into daily conflict.

The white women learnt the rough language of the locals. Ballroom dancing and curated gowns stitched by expert tailors hid the hard life they led. Travelling to India facing the heat and the dust they followed their husbands or fiancés to set up a home in inhospitable areas. Many died of malaria and diarrhoea at a very young age. Gravestones mark their sad stories.

Gravestones mention the sad reasons. The officers led from the front and traversed difficult terrains to set up garrisons and regiments. Lansdowne is no exception; named after Lord Lansdowne who was then the Viceroy of India. It is a hill station in the north Indian state of Uttarakhand. It was founded as a military garrison under the British Raj in 1887.

Lansdowne is unlike other hill stations. It has well connected motorable roads but remote in its own way. It is situated in the Pauri Garhwal district of Uttarakhand. At an altitude of 1780 mts above sea level surrounded with thick oak and blue pine forests, its scenic beauty draws many tourists seeking a quiet holiday. 245 kms by road from Delhi, the winter season temperature ranges from 4 degrees to 15 degrees. The whole town is canvassed in pale whites of snow.

One of the most decorated infantry regiments of the Indian Army the Garhwal Rifles was originally raised here in 1887 as the 39th (Garhwal) Regiment of the Bengal Army. It then became part of the British Indian Army, and after the Independence of India, it was incorporated into the Indian Army. Written in bold letters across the wall that encloses the training centre are the words, "Abode of the Veer Garhwali". Mainly made up of Garhwali soldiers, this regiment has a distinguished record and a unique identity. The regimental insignia incorporates a Maltese Cross and is based on the defunct Rifle Brigade (Prince Consort's Own) as they are a designated rifle regiment. Unlike regular rifle regiments, they are one of 10 such units marching in the regular paces used in Indian Army's ceremonies.

The army mess is an incredible memento of the past. The walls are decorated with the stuffed heads of various mountain animals hunted by the English *sahebs*. Heads of antlers, bears, boars, *neel gais*, *bisons*, tigers, leopards, lions, and elephants are mounted on wooden plaques. They seem to line up in silence of over a hundred years. They speak aloud the horrific pillaging of the forests and its creatures by the coloniser. They have been preserved not as trophies but to tell us the story of the grandeur of wildlife that inhabited these regions of Garhwal. It is a call for protecting our ecology, Our forests.

Sunder Lal Bahuguna the renowned eco activist and leader of the *chipko* movement to save forests belonged to Garhwal. The billiard room, the ball room and the dining hall are polished and shining. One chair at the dining table is always vacant with the crockery and cutlery set out for the dinner. It is believed that the ghost guest (a missing officer) occupies it. Just nobody has ever broken the custom.

Lansdowne is a very quiet place. Those looking for fun time, fast food and restaurants are sorely disappointed. There are no fun places, bustling markets or touristic restaurants like in most popular hill stations. No quaint streets either. Its very isolation is its attraction. There is a sense of Time having stopped somewhere in these hills, chapels and churches made of grey stone stand witness to a vibrant military life that throbbed here a century and a half ago. Grand and great grandchildren of British officers who served in these terrains visit and have written interesting blogs one can read on the internet. These stories connect us to a real time. Photographs from the past authenticate their presence.

We walked up to St Mary's Church built during the colonial period made of grey stones with a large bell hanging outside. Its quaintness is most attractive. My mind travelled to the past re-imaging the sahibs and memsahibs, all formally dressed attending the church service; miles away from their homes in England trying hard to carry out Imperial instructions. Mussoorie, the Garhwali's read by the British trained from a curious name like Tip-n-Top viewpoint, we could see why Lansdowne is well-known for its scenic beauty, weather, and peaceful surroundings. One can savour the enchanting views of the Himalayas with majestic sunrise and sunset from different viewpoints. The *Chaukhamba* and Trishul peaks of the Garhwal Himalayas are visible from here. The sunset is stunning. Ironically, the sun had long set on the British Empire.

First published in e-journal Different Truths. Edited by Mr. Arindam Roy and Ms Anumita Roy

Rupa Rao

Down The Memory Lane

My rich childhood is a colourful mosaic replete with magical moments that make me smile decades later, continents away from home. As newlyweds parents began their life at YOLE near Dharamsala- Dalai Lama land and conceived their first born.

My Dad was an AMC doctor and we children loved to tag along at the tender ages of 4 plus to go "visit" new born babies in the Military hospital at Dehu Road near Pune where young dad was then posted. We families in the Indian army pride ourselves at the camaraderie, kinship regardless of rank and file when it comes to any important life events.

An officer or a *jawaan* as a new dad is no different; we would gaze at the miracle of a newborn and share in the excitement of new parents with grandparents who joined them for the delivery. *Mithaai* served by "sweeper" trade personnel or otherwise made no difference (which was still a social stigma back in the days where in weird small ways casteism reared its head quietly).

We had millions of small and big adventures in our black ambassador car driven by a small built but larger than life personality dad, he managed nonstop drives single handedly with devotion and love. We traversed Assam to AP and back or From Punjab depending on where we were posted. Once we were driving through the dreaded chambal valley infested with killer dacoits of fame, and police stopped us warning us about the risks. Our brave dad said no dacoit will harm a fauji; and he was right; while our palpitating hearts in our mouths were praying he drove on through deserted roads alone in the dark night.

We had umpteen impromptu family picnics in this big family car, singing songs all through the drives. Stopping to pick mangoes or seasonal produce to enjoy and later distribute amongst friends. We had to cross "*sukhwaa-dukhwaa* Dam" once, and the swollen water was gushing, we were sure we all would be washed away; dad made us alight, cross over, then drove through the rushing currents to safety. Our lives mattered more to our courageous dad.

Swim in the Abohar water canal near Fazilka was heavenly cool; and close to the borders while dad and many others lived in trenches and bunkers.

Ferozepur's separated family home while dad was away on field post was barely 5-8 miles away from Pak and we could hear odd gunshots. No alarms were raised but all were vigilant. Ever ready for adventures dad and always supportive mom that magically whipped fun food in moments gave us memories of a lifetime that linger on.

As we grew into high-schoolers, a three-ton truck ferried us students from MHOW to Indore, closest HS at Central school for the transferrable army lot like us. We cherished the not too smooth rides of over an hour each way daily, with a flapping tarpaulin in front to protect us from blazing summer heat, monsoon showers or the chilly temperatures and winds in winters. Unforgettable exchanges, laughter, fights, crushes, love letters, some bullying too was part of the ride till we became one with this close-knit family. No outsider was allowed to intrude in ways that hurt this group, was beautiful.

Rau was a small town between home and school where an occasional stop to spend saved up paisa afforded us "*Rau ki Kachori*" that made our eyes water and tongues burn but I still swear I have never eaten a better kachori in life ever.

Simplicity, naivete was the trademark where we all wished every adult a "good morning or evening or night" without fail; I recall my maternal aunt called that "artificial" which hurt then.

We had a limited number of civil clothing as school uniforms simplified the complexities of differences for most part. It was no shame to repeat clothing often as most sported the same sans shame as is the case today where burgeoning wardrobes would put Imelda Carlos collection to shame.

When dad drove us to Jabalpur hostel after 12th grade, an amazing family of Col Puri aunty uncle became our local guardians who would take us home, feed us yummy home food and drop us back. Day out was a gift to hostel-bound youth who missed parents posted at odd locations.

Taking a train to travel to Pachmarhi , a picturesque beautiful town in the mountains meant changing trains, and requesting a ride from the army rep at the railway station to surprise parents-yet it was all so safe and kosher. Air travel was not even a close option, possibly unaffordable to us those days altogether.

Homes were huge British relics with amazing bungalows that boasted of stables, sprawling lawns, and bedrooms with bathrooms one could drown in.

Entertaining was a staple on almost daily basis where one or more army families gathered over tea, or dinner to break bread; children played on their own and adults had CSD canteen Rum or whisky for most part, if it was daytime then likely Beer or Gin was the choice. Children gorged on Fanta, Gold Spot, Coke as per the availability. Rasna and sherbet were often added to the list. Fried snack in the evening was heavenly to accompany the drinks.

Mother had Ladies club meets where they shared more than tea and talks, it was a session on some art, craft, recipe which bonded them all as one family and was an occasion to dress up for girl time away from the serving armed personnel spouses.

Mess food during visits, transfers; temporary tiny accommodations were like a warm blanket and adjusting, accommodating came with much ease each time we moved Punjab to Assam, UP, MP, AP, or beautiful J&K, Manipur, etc.

In Jhansi our home faced the huge parade grounds and seeing everyone gather in uniform and march, meet, mingle was a matter of pride. White stones there were fodder for big sister to spin tales of Lilliputs who lived inside them and came alive at her calling; we all were ardent followers who believed her yarns with adoration and fear.

When our 52-year grandmother passed away from cancer, officers, *jawaans* came immediately to support dad and mom. Everyone stood there offering support; even the entire school staff with principal Mr G Ram and teachers landed up in the school bus to offer condolences.

There is glitz, glamor attached to army life but there is a lot more behind it where dads, brothers, sons are lost to time in sacrifice for the country. All through transfers, multiple moves, new bonding, new geographical posts, new schools and cultures and people, what stayed the same was the family feeling amongst children and families of officers and jawaans alike who shared lives, times, bread, stories, playtimes together sans differences.

Rootlessness gives a resilience and adaptability; acceptance and non-judgement is a staple by osmosis. I am proud to have had the privileges of those decades of untouched pride amongst those who care for our country above all. Patriotic slogans, songs were not mere words, they were imbibed sentiments having witnessed love, loss, mortality, valour, discipline, sacrifice, pain, separations, celebration all at once without realizing how the highest priority was and is our nation.

Sahana Ahmed

Love Stories

I had fallen hard; I should have taken my time getting up. I didn't know the status of my tailbone yet, but my plans lay shattered. I was on my way to Gangtok, on a personal pilgrimage of sorts, to relive the best years of my youth. Having grown up in the army, being part of a community of drifters, I was likelier to have reunions with places than people, and Gangtok was my teenage crush. Which is why slipping near a waterfall, straight into the water, was a huge dampener, pun not intended.

Now I was worried I would not be able to climb the stairs in Lal Bazaar, or endure the trek to my old home in Burtuk. I was worried I would have to skip Palzor Stadium, and Penengla, and my school too. I wanted, so badly, to meet Gangtok, but I could hardly walk two steps without wincing. There was a time when I could conquer the steepest of stairwells – and they are ubiquitous in Gangtok – without breaking a sweat. The memory of those days was still alive in my legs and so, there was hope still. My classmate, Sonal, had once counted the number of steps we climbed each day. Almost one thousand. Our school was in the valley, in the cantonment, four kilometres from the bus stop. We would rush down the hills in the morning, for our bus was always late, and what wonderful names those buses had! Shaan-e-Sikkim, Lachung Mail, Khatara... The first two were plush, almost luxurious, with big windows through which floated in thick mist (which then disappeared into the mouths of the less shy). Music played on the speakers, mostly Bollywood, sometimes Bhojpuri, whenever the driver with the handlebar *moochh* was on duty. There were so many songs that I first heard on the way to school. I still remember the grey, drizzly morning when I was hit by the beauty of 1942: A Love Story...

After school, Sonal and I used to run up the road to grab window seats. We had devised a way to beat the others. We would run and chant, sometimes made-up words, the rhythm growing faster and faster till we were practically flying. Our feet loved the challenge; it always worked!

It was the magic of those carefree days that I wanted to relive. It was that magic that I tried to capture in my first book. Unlike my protagonist, I never D-A-T-E-D a boy who made my heart flutter like prayer flags in the wind, who whistled *pahadi dhuns* while the Kanchenjunga blushed. I wish I had. What fun it would have been: to make all the aunties go psst psst, to make the (impossibly fashionable) local girls go green-green-eyed. I wish I knew a boy from Mayo who could make the TNA boys give me a second look. I wish I did. Alas, all that did not happen. All the boys fell for Sonal. I was left with stories.

a new favourite

writer I know writes to know

what she is thinking

Sanjeev Sethi

Barrack Backgrounder

As the scions of cadres from cantonment,
we cycled and dog-paddled across channels
of peradventure. In differences, we dwelled
to witness the idea of India. Circa 1971.
December 3, while aircrafts flitted through
Agra, in blackout, we were invited to pre-
planned at-home by a Major from Mizoram:
her son's seventh. In tenebrosity, she offered
*bhatooras but no *chole. We grokked aunty
had gone wrong, in a whiz stillness gagged us.
One of us whispered ketchup and our carousal
grooved to another level of bonhomie as
airships gargled.

*Indian meal combo: eating one without the other
is an incomplete experience.

Snatch Of Schooldays

A three-tonner transported us, shaking its way through crosscuts and corridors of the cantonment. It was an honorable way to hightail. As with all things army, punctuality was the praxis. Kids weren't keyed into it. On erring the local bus was my burrow. From my headset, these were expeditions. I snaked my way contiguous to the leadfoot, locus of the exit. There were other straphangers. All rooted for him, laughed at one-liners, supported his silliness. Influence of being in the driver's seat came early.

Seema Ahira

The Price Of Peace

Friends and family gather
To celebrate the jubilant return
Of the soldier from the battle field
Tired, a bit on the skinny side but in one piece

Generous drinks were poured
Copious amounts of food flowed
Music played into the wee hours of the night
And we danced until exhaustion set

Everyone clamoured for a picture
And they were willingly obliged
Gallantry could not be abandoned
Even in the face of extreme enervation

An indiscernible sadness
In those deeply set eyes
A nauseous blend of guilt and melancholia
That had forever stained the psyche

The dour hue could never be washed
Digging in its heals refusing to be scoured
Try as I may to cleanse
And wipe it with contrition

The relentless squall of gunfire
The thud of falling bodies
The sickening gurgle of comrades
Choking and drowning in their own blood

The harrowing face of war
The lingering nightmare
Unseen wounds that fester
Long after we return to our quarter

We have subdued the enemy
But the foe within is unscathed
Precarious peace at our borders
Comes at a high personal price

This Is Goodbye

The quite pride we take
To serve our nation... our motherland
Often hides what is left unsaid

The unspoken fears...for our children on the front
Unshed tears for those that have not returned
And mourning for those that are left behind

The heavy heart of the newlywed
Bidding a soulful goodbye with hennaed hands
Not knowing when she will hear from her beloved next

The soldiers stoic demeanour
Drilled into his very fabric
Belies the angst revealed by his eyes

To serve and protect
No matter the personal cost
Is the motto this is never lost

On the brave harts that serve on the front lines
The families that await their return
And a nation that celebrates their valour

Shyamola Khanna

For Pragya Bajpai: Teaching Recruited Soldiers

From kindergarten to Business school, I have taught at all levels whenever I have had the opportunity. I have enjoyed myself and I know that my audience has been equally entertained and probably learnt something!

But this present stint with recruited soldiers is another ball game altogether. They are coming from the hinterlands and the government schools therein. They are going to be the clerical staff at all the army offices across the country.

Let me give you a peep as to what is going on in their minds.

The soldier is happy he has a *sarkari* job. His whole lifestyle has changed. There he was in the village: sleeping till all odd hours, watching movies, eating what his mother lovingly made for the *"suputra"* (the good son) while the father yelled and screamed and called him *'nikamma'*(useless!)

Post the enrolment, the boys have been through the grind: Wake up at 0400 hrs, go for a run, exercise etc for the next hour plus. Return to the lines for shit, shave and shampoo, head for breakfast. By this time, they are so hungry they could collectively eat a horse! Sure!

The Army feeds them well and they can eat all they want. By 0800 hrs they are in the training battalion, cleaning their classrooms and the area all around, under the strict supervision of the instructors (subedars and havaldars) with powerful voices. They don't need any crowd hailers!

The discipline is physically taxing but you do not see any soldier straying. Of course, English Grammar can put the devil to sleep so I do excuse some of them when they start dozing off.

Some of them are soldiers' sons who have been through Kendriya Vidyalayas and are fairly well spoken and eager to learn.

But one thing is sure, they have not met any teachers like Shahnaz Sharif (a total Grammar nazi) and me; both wives of IAF officers. Amazingly no Army wife has stepped into this domain.

Their perspective of us is as much an eye opener as any other. They have never had teachers who insisted on their speaking English for the little time they are with us. They have not come across so much of grammar and reading and writing of English. They have never looked at a dictionary.

Then our persona! Both of us wear pants and kurtas etc, none of the traditional teachers' sari clad looks! That and our addressing them as *'puttar'* or son gives us the slight motherly touch! So along with helping them learn some spoken and written English, we do our best with teaching them somethings about body language, attitude, and personality. Of course, the interest in such matters perks up when we talk of marriage, love, and girlfriends! I doubt if any adult has ever spoken to them about such matters!

A recent discussion on the Agniveer scheme of the Government of India revealed a different perspective. Some of them thought that the idea of working with a lump sum of money (the kind they have never seen!) was a challenge and they felt that they could try. Some felt that the Agniveer would not be able to get married as the girls' families always wanted a permanent job for their future sons-in-law! Sad perspective indeed. It meant that there was no faith in the intrinsic capability of the young person.

Or is it lack of exposure? Or is it the lethargy generated by the pension schemes?

When a man retires from active government service, he feels he is entitled to rest and recuperate., after having earned his pension. It is time to change the narrative and the perspective. Given the better medical facilities and better health care today, people are living longer and can contribute to society in myriad other ways.

When I pointed it out to my soldier boys that they probably have a father or grandfather lolling around on a charpoy and ordering the wife or the daughter-in-law to get them this, that or the other! Some of them had sheepish grins on their faces!

I did tell them that India is the only country where all government servants get pension, including the PM and the President, while in the western (developed) world there is no pension at all for anyone!

Shahnaz had done a lesson on the writing of agenda and minutes. So, the day ended with their writing down the minutes of what we had discussed in class. I could hear the subdued groans and moans! Why? Why do we have to write it down?

Reminds me of my 12-year-old grandson and his online Hindi lesson! "I will read it out to you Nani, why do I have to write it down? Please Nani! Don't torture me!"

The Semi-Literate Teacher

Kavitha sits on a cot under the neem tree, surrounded by the three kids she is teaching. The kids are repeating loudly what she has told them to. While I watch amused, she comes to me to ask what was written in the oldest child's diary.

More than twenty years ago, her parents had come to stay as our domestic help. Kavitha's father was a driver and an alcoholic. I tried to get Kavitha and her brother Venkatesh enrolled in a government school. I took their lessons, and both worked hard, with a lot of scolding and punishments from me. Then Kavitha started her periods and the whole world turned topsy turvy. She was barely 12 going on 13. The family packed up and left for the village where they performed the wedding rituals. She was married off to a cousin she detested. All my protests fell on deaf ears.

School came to an unceremonious end for both the sister and brother. Six months later the little girl was back. I spotted her sitting on the steps of the house across the road. I asked the mother what happened? No explanations, except sheer embarrassment that she had let the parents down by running away from her marriage. The father and mother began beating her with sticks and stones-- I was amazed that she survived.

Some 15 years later Kavitha, Venkatesh and their mother came back to stay in my servant's quarters. A lot had happened in their lives—the father had finally kicked the bucket. Venkatesh was now a driver with a valid license and a job. Kavitha came with an infant, a few months old. Her 'husband' was in Dubai. Slowly, ever so slowly, her story unfolded.

She had been working in a store and doing pretty well. There she met Anand who had been her neighbour for a very long time. They fell in love, and she decided to marry him, knowing full well that he was already married and had a teenaged son. There were no fancy wedding trappings this time, no registration, no acknowledgement by the parents. But she was happy.

Very soon she was pregnant and despite her husband's protests she went ahead and had the baby. Since she did not obey his diktat, he left her to her own devices, occasionally providing her some money. When the little boy was two, Kavitha found herself pregnant again—her husband had been visiting her on the quiet. Her brother, Venkatesh, who was helping her run the household put his foot down and insisted she abort the foetus. Thankfully, she heard him out and with the help of a doctor she managed to free herself of this additional burden. Her husband meanwhile continues to abandon his responsibility while she is making sure her little boy goes to school. Venkatesh's wife had decided to leave for the village with his two kids. She has since returned.

Kavitha is a mothering sort and insists that the three kids—her brother's two and her own one--- study. She is ferrying them to and from the school. She has even been in a minor accident, but she does not give up. Kavitha is street smart; she knows how to order stuff online; she can handle her bank accounts and is a quick learner on the phone computer. She has learnt how to sew clothes and is making some pin money on the side. She has understood that she must look after herself. Her mother remains her biggest support.

Siddhant Kaushal

Riches Of A Legacy

Being the grandson of an Army officer has shaped my personality in many ways. I was in the 7th grade when my Nana passed away but the time I spent with him is the time I cherish the most. Looking back I remember how he always kept me close to him, so I picked up many of his values unknowingly.

He was a disciplined man and followed a strict routine. He would always say, "Routine is boring but can do wonders for you later in life." It was his decision, along with that of my parents, to send me to a boarding school. Today, I realise how all his decisions helped me discipline myself, adjust, and survive during the different phases of my life.

As a kid I remember him asking me once, "What is 1+1?" and I immediately said 2.

He asked, "Are you sure?"

I said yes, to which he said, "No it's not 2, it is 11."

Being a little kid, I blurted out, "Nana your teachers haven't taught you well, you should re-join school with me." He laughed loudly and heartily. I still can't get that laughter out of my head.

Then he said, "Always try and challenge things and think out of the box. Don't fall into the trap called-*'this is how it is'*. Asking questions is very good. You should challenge and learn."

I guess that stuck somewhere in my subconscious; only later in life I realised how his words helped shape my personality. He, along with my Nani exposed me to a lot of folk music, as my mom would take us to our village Ramgarh, in Phillaur, during our vacations. We had family gatherings and all my cousins, and the extended family would come together to celebrate. We needed no special occasion or festival to share joy, love, and togetherness.

Everyone, my cousins, and even the neighbours around would get together and sing 'Tappe', 'Boliyaan', and many other folk songs.

My Nani who never had any formal education but was the most street-smart person around always gave the best bits of advice. I think she was the most intelligent one in the family. She could do anything and everything.

She and Nana taught us the importance of getting together as a family, festivals were only an excuse. I see their traits in my mother also and she has always passed on these qualities to us. Like my Nana, my mom always tells me to follow my heart, to never look back. She has always taught me to have no regrets in life. She has been my biggest support in whatever I do today. Whenever I feel low, she being a fauji's daughter knows exactly how to lift my spirits, along with her maternal love.

Today I try and carry forward this legacy in my own little way by doing the things they taught me and the wisdom they have passed on to me.

Sujata Parashar

Grey

Sky has given way
to a bewitching shade of grey.
Grey they say is dull and dark.
The one I witnessed is seductive instead;
carrying dollops of hope
and a bowl of lazy teasing smile.

There's something more on the grey plate;
Soft, fluffy and rare
It smells like vanilla with a hint of musk and amber
but the flavour's unknown.

Perhaps we shall know the taste when the sky descends…
You are the reason for the arresting shade of grey
I'm the spice finely hidden
in the pouring rain.

Sunil Kaushal

Goodbyes!

Excerpt From Gypsy Wanderings –Part 2

My husband passed over on 12th January 2023. Having grown up under the secular influence of four generations in the army, my children unquestioningly followed instructions by the pandit ji conducting the cremation rites according to the practiced routine that allowed no space for personal emotions. Typical of the patriarchal hegemony as practised in Hinduism and to different degrees by other religions as well, both my sons and young grandson were to perform the rites while my daughter was not even considered.

When they were asked to place wood on his burning pyre, I let my daughter and granddaughter to do the same. It was no rebellious act; only an affirmation of my own beliefs and values that I have always proclaimed and advocated; an honouring of my husband's values in bringing up his daughter like his sons, and an honouring of my mother's memory.

Many questions and significant memories from my childhood stirred, when my mother, a fauji wife, handled death totally differently, when her father expired, ignoring tradition way back in 1950.

Daddy was posted at Meerut at that time. Then in her early thirties, Mummy chose to live in the remote countryside with four small children, so they could be educated in the best schools of the country at Dehra Doon, while Daddy served his motherland.

Clement Town was a picturesque little cantonment nestled in the sylvan surroundings of the Doon valley at the foothills of the Himalayas. Sparsely populated, the residents were mostly army personnel working in the Service Selection Board and the Joint Services Wing (JSW), some retired officers, a few Anglo-

Indians, and some British people who chose to stay back in India. Bungalows far apart were connected by dirt roads. The only telephone was in the postage stamp-sized post office, three miles from Summer House, our home.

After my grandmother's death, Naana ji preferred to live with us in Clement Town, Dehra Doon, instead of either of his three sons. Breaking patriarchal dominance runs in my family since ages.

That day my grandfather had high fever due to pneumonia. The only doctor was five miles away. Our gardener, who ran to fetch him, rode on the carrier as the doctor cycled down. He gave my grandfather a Penicillin shot, some aspirin and left. Within a few minutes, my grandfather was no more. Allergic reaction to penicillin was probably not yet known.

It was afternoon but the wintry sun was already wrapping up its watered-down warmth, with a chilly wind chasing small foggy wisps around. The only cremation ground was nine miles away in Dehra Doon.

The cook and one of the gardeners laid Naana ji's body on the floor, covered with a sheet. My sister, Didi and I, draped garlands of his favourite roses on his body. My younger brother and I hardly understood what had happened.

Another gardener fetched a taxi. Bhaji, my elder brother and he sat in front. Mummy, at the back, cradled her father's head in her lap, his body on the seat. Consigning his mortal remains to the setting sun, flames reduced dust to dust once again, the spirit having flown.

There was no electricity as our bungalow was still under construction. The cook lit the kerosene lamps as usual and cooked dinner. Mummy reached home around nine and slumped on the floor near Naana's bed. Tired and overwhelmed, courage succumbed to grief, as our dog Whiskey snuggling up, placed her head on Mummy's lap, their tears intermingling.

Daddy reached on the third day. Both immersed his ashes in a nearby river. When her brothers reached on the fourth day, as a family they all chanted prayers from the Guru Granth Sahib and the last rites were over.

Mummy had no barriers to cremating her father, seventy-three years ago. Sikhism holds no gender discrimination, although aberrations do take place sometimes when cultural lines get blurred.

Sadly, the clock has rewound centuries back. Today we still cling to rituals that strip women of many rights in the name of religious and societal pressure, but are based on patriarchal suppression, even when women shatter many a glass ceiling.

How Daddy had inculcated a sense of independence in his young unschooled wife, I discovered through an old letter of his, written from Palestine, at my birth. He was then serving under the British Army during WWII. Besides his joy and excitement over having a second daughter, is a paragraph insisting that I be given the name he liked, Sunil. He spared no chance to break gender biases. This long letter about different family matters repeatedly told Mummy to take decisions according to her own understanding and wisdom.

As a fauji wife, Mummy was well prepared to take over the toughest task in the event of any domestic exigencies and had autonomous rights over all matters, be it family, health, finances, property, or our education. She proved her mettle and often rose in stature, heads above trained and literate people.

It was this confidence, instilled in her by Daddy, and years of an army backdrop, that enabled her to make a place as a pioneer exporter of ethnic garments to Germany, in her seventies. This unschooled woman rose to win the President's award through the Export Promotion Council for ten years.

The armed forces do not train just their soldiers. The women, children, and aged parents left behind, learn to fend for themselves, with fortitude and resilience. The credit goes to both the men and women, working as a team, the soldiers trust the women to do their best, often single-handed, and the women hold the fort with the freedom to make decisions.

Swati Pal

My Heart Wears Olive Green

One of the first things I remember about my childhood is singing the song, "The life in the army, they say is mighty fine, you ask for soda whiskey, they give you turpentine....' and so on! It would always be sung with great gusto and accompanied with peals of laughter. No matter if the times were troubled, no matter if your dad/ son/ brother/ mother/ sister/ wife were at the warfront or in a field area, when songs like this were sung, there was no dearth of merriment. Resilience, courage, a positive spirit, and the power of a smile- these were lessons I learnt early as an 'army brat'- the umbrella term for all fauji kids!

And then there are the cantt areas. Cantonments are a world of their own. Even today when I enter a cantt area, I feel a sense of great familiarity and nostalgia. The green everywhere from the well mown grass along roads, the office areas and in the private gardens of residents; the riot of colourful flowers peeping out from every nook and cranny; very old, gnarled trees especially fruit bearing ones; the sleepy quietness of summer afternoons spent on the white woven garden chairs; the immaculate cleanliness; the well-marked roads; the Unit signages with their battle cries; often, one odd iron statue of a soldier or a tank placed at a prominent spot; and of course, the culverts on which I spent so much time with my friends! If I were to define paradise on earth, it would have to be a Cantonment!

I don't know if it is a coincidence or whether my father planned it that way, but after my birth, Baba was posted to the 'field postings'. Family, including spouse is unable to accompany the officer to the field area generally because of difficult conditions with inadequate facilities. And so the family lives in what are called 'separated family quarters'. The word 'separated' conjures up so much hardship involved and certainly, it was not at all easy with husband/father so far away. But my memories of the long spell in the huge, separated family quarters at Lucknow Cantt are only good ones. It was a huge colony and each manned by the wife of the officer gone away. What an immense sisterhood I saw in my childhood, a community of strong women who were always there for each other and faced joy and adversity together. How wonderfully we all adapted to 'managing' things on our own and the incredible amount we learnt from each other. My Mom's friends taught her so many different cuisines ranging from biryani to meat loaf and what a time we families would have breaking bread together! Impromptu get-togethers were ever so common where the principle of potluck was at work, and we relished every morsel.

All of these may give the impression that things were simply splendid all the time but it's not so. I have memories of my dad getting his first heart attack when he was posted to a field area. There was no phone in our house and information about his health would reach the Commandant only via a special signal in the evening. We would trudge to his house every day and wait till the signal came. We were so terrified. Yet everyone rallied around and thus the time passed.

And it is this standing by each other that my memories always go back to. That's what life as an army child taught me. As it is said about those who wear the olive green, that one remains a soldier even after laying down the uniform, so may it be said about me, that I will ever be a loyal fauji at heart!

Tanushree Poddar

The Writer Within

Excerpt From a Conversation with Pragya Bajpai

When I was married to an army officer, I was working as a human resources executive in a large multinational company in Delhi. With the marriage came a crucial question of whether I would continue with my career or accompany my husband to wherever he was posted.

I quit my job. There were two factors that played a role in my decision. First, after working for 8 years in the corporate sector, the demanding job stopped exciting me. Second, I loved writing. For a long time, I had been freelancing for various newspapers and magazines, and now it was time to devote my energies to writing. I listened to the call of my heart.

My husband's postings took us through the length and breadth of the country. We travelled to places I had never heard of. I love nature and the thrill of adventure, so I didn't miss city life. There were difficulties, of course, but I loved the challenge of setting up a home in the strangest of places. Whether it was the wilderness of Hathigorh, a small town in Rajasthan, or a nature-kissed Himalayan town, I loved each place. There were many interesting experiences, and they taught me many lessons.

Army wives are resilient, courageous, and multi-tasking individuals. Whether her husband is posted to far-flung areas, or he is fighting terrorists, she learns to take the highs with the lows. She handles the practical day-to-day requirements, often holds a job, brings up the children, and has to maintain a smiling and cheerful front. When the husband is at the border or in the valley, she goes through living death every single day, but she doesn't have the luxury of wallowing in worry. All this requires a lot of mental and emotional strength.

Those lessons made me realize that the contribution of army wives remains unsung; she is that pillar that makes it possible for the husband to do his job without worrying about his family. It is her job to ensure that he remains stress-free as far as the family is concerned.

I learned to deal with the challenges of being an army wife. In the meantime, I continued to write whenever I found the time to do so. There was no computer or internet in those days. I had a portable typewriter, and I wrote short stories, travelogues, and articles for magazines. I had to post hard copies of my writings by snail mail, and it took weeks to hear from the editors. Meantime, I continued with the activities expected of an army wife.

I wrote whatever caught my fancy. Humour, I discovered, was my forte. Hundreds of 'middles' in almost all national newspapers followed. Then, the constant human urge to conquer new frontiers took me to travel writing. Both my husband and I love traveling, so we travelled whenever possible, and I wrote about our experiences. A romance with all kinds of writing - from political satire and interviews to book reviews and serious articles continued in between.

The transition from writing short stories to books took place soon after. My flirtation with books began with nonfiction and I tested unfamiliar grounds. I grappled with the complexities of the publishing industry. Initially, I was baffled by the legal terms in contracts, royalty statements, and figures. Roadblocks were aplenty, but I took tiny steps across new frontiers. I stumbled and fell, and then I got up, dusted myself, and started all over again.

I wrote over a dozen non-fiction books. Then, it was time to step into the world of fiction, and I did so with enthusiasm.

My first book, *Boots Belts Berets*, dealt with the lives of NDA (National Defence Academy) cadets. I wrote it as a tribute to the army officers who had passed through the hallowed portals of the prestigious institute. In the meantime, I wrote Nurjahan's Daughter, which was set in the Mughal period. The readers and the critics liked both the books. Encouraged by the response, I continued to write.

Then, I was invited to the IMA (Indian Military Academy) to address the gentlemen cadets. They asked me why I hadn't written a book on the IMA. Their question made me write *On the Double*, which is about GCs (Gentlemen Cadets) in the IMA. The same thing happened when I met some women officers. They asked me why I hadn't written a book about them. *The Girls in Green* was written to pay a tribute to the women in the Indian army.

People think of soldiers as strong and valiant characters, who are forever ready to lay their lives in the line of fire. They forget soldiers are not robots, but human beings. Like every other person, they also have their fears and insecurities. They have their share of joys, sorrows, and heartbreaks. They also have a love life. My military books take readers through all those factors.

Writing on any subject requires in-depth knowledge of the same. One can't make mistakes, at least not where facts are concerned. It is one reason outsiders find it difficult to write about army life. To that extent, as an army wife, I have an advantage. I have had the opportunity of observing the details at a close range for many years.

During interviews, I am often asked why I don't stick to one genre. I think it would bore me to write in a single genre, so I write about subjects that make me curious and throw up a challenge or one that rouses a strong feeling in me. I wrote Death of a Dictator–the Story of Saddam Hussein after the US invasion of Iraq because I was so angry about the invasion. My concerns about climate change resulted in *Decoding the Feronia Files.*

I have written in the military, historical, crime, adventure, and supernatural genres. Writing in these genres has given me an opportunity to research and learn about various things. They have opened up my mind and widened my perspective. I feel that the greatest challenge in writing a book is to find a strong storyline and a credible protagonist. Once that is in place, it becomes a writer's job to hold the readers' interest till the last page, and that is the biggest challenge. Writing gives me a reason to live. It is my oxygen.

Toolika Rani

Connection

It wasn't until the ray arrived,
It wasn't until the day arrived
That I saw the life,
In a different light.
The fulcrum upon which I hung,
Rotated around my own axis,
Even the slightest crack hurt.
Hostage of my own spin,
My world view converged,
To a centripetal point,
To a point of no return,
Where things couldn't be worse.
Startled I awoke,
At the dread it evoked,
At the fall it enlisted,
At the myth it had busted.
In the hell of dejection,
Roamed so many of them,
Suddenly I realized,
I wasn't so alone!
I wasn't so alone in the quagmire of pain,
I wasn't so alone clasped to my chain,
That collective gloom became my strength,
I wasn't to die; I was to wrench,

The wretched from the pain.
It swirled and swirled ferociously in my brain,
The radiance it burst,
I found my weapon,
I caught the train,
Of thoughts, hopes, linked with the grain,
of human connection, and deep passion,
emerging from me to the millions of those,
whom above me, I finally chose.

The Rising Tide

Plunging into the depth of the ocean,
the tide bemoaned her fate,
"Oh! The downfall!"
The crushing sound of falling to the floor,
My rising glory, the days of yore.
My waters that pulled a force on the moon,
My beauty over which millions would swoon,
I rose like a wall, fierce and tall,
Who could have imagined,
this devastating fall!
No more a spectacular sight to behold,

I am now mere drops, what a pity to be told!
"Take heart O' child!
Don't feel so morose"
I am where you bloomed,
Now listen up and close!
Your glory and the grief,
both would be brief,
I gave them to you,
and I would retrieve.
While on the rise,
you witnessed the heights,
experienced delight,
but that is only half of the slice,
which is called life!

Submerged in me,
experience the pain,
so that you may,
appreciate your gain.
Come out of your self-centred misery,
Observe the world a little more wisely,
All around you
the waves rise and fall,
completing a circle,
however small.
Whatever goes up,
is destined to come down,
but that doesn't mean,
its fervour will drown.
There will be a rising tide again,
collect your drops,
the process of reconstruction,
has already began.

I, the ocean, never cease to flow,
So, you my child, are bound to grow,
Gather your forces from far and wide,
You will again be called,
The Rising Tide!

Tulika Niyogi
Mountain Trail

Those were the days when my husband was posted to Ranikhet, a beautiful hill station located in the northern part of India. As the name goes, indeed it appeared 'queen of valleys' with picturesque surroundings, snow clad mountain peaks, spiral roads, greenery, and breath-taking views from all corners of the town.

We had a daily routine to go for our walks in the evening. It used to fill up our hearts with gratitude for the Mother Nature when the Sun went down gradually in between the trees, reflecting it's aura and light with a promise of abundance of happiness and more sunshine the following days!

It was a wonderful feeling and we used to stand occasionally to absorb the beauty with our heart and soul!

On that day, we got out little late. It was chilly outside, so we wrapped ourselves comfortably and started climbing up towards a new location, at a little higher altitude called "Chaubatia"! The road was steep and after a while I was feeling warm. We were slow but steady. There was this atypical aroma of Pine and Deodar trees, which gave a soothing effect.

We never realised that it was getting dark faster, and roads ahead appeared foggy slowly. Streetlights were placed quite at a distance from one another, and vehicles were plying less and so were the pedestrians. We were standing at a 'hair pin' bend to decide whether we should proceed ahead towards the 'unknown'!

I was thirsty and wanted to sit somewhere to relax for a while. So much of quietness was there and we were little flabbergasted! Suddenly we saw some movements in the bushes afar. The broken twigs of trees and dried leaves were crushed upon. A bright light of torch fell on us and we got panicked.

Two of our soldiers with their jungle uniforms on, were right in front of us. "JAI HIND SAAAAB"! They greeted us in unison, with heavy tapping sounds of their high-ankled boots!

"Aagey paidal mat jaiye! Andhere mein cheetah nikalta hai"! (Don't go ahead walking! Leopards come out in the dark!) We shivered and felt the goosebumps! We had heard about the mountain leopards, spotted sometimes around the dense slopes.

We were so relieved to see "our saviour guards "on patrol duty! They accompanied us till we reached down to a busy area. We were at loss of words to thank them from the core of our hearts. It was a matter to ponder while we were heading towards home:-

"On those barred, narrow mountain roads

When it's dark and cold

Wilderness around

With some bizarre sounds

YOU are there without a sigh

The heavily dressed , 'military guy'

Facing ALL situations, odd or even

Always prompt to serve people or nation

Because of YOU, we are safe

We are assured, Because YOU are brave

We enjoy the comforts of our home

While YOU are the defender, all alone

For we live well, YOU are ready to die

YOU even leave, without saying goodbye!"

I felt small cold drops on my cheeks,

and eyes became blurred. Wiping my face with the handkerchief,

I looked up at the starlit sky!

Albeit we are the luckiest ones to inhale chest full!!!

Vidisha Kaushal

A Grand-Daughter Speaks

Integrity, loyalty, duty, respect, selfless service, courage, and honour, most of us recognize these as core values of the army. I witnessed these at close range throughout my childhood years, spent with my grandparents.

On one hand, Nana as we lovingly called him was the epitome of discipline and consistency; on the other, he was also a doting grandfather and a caring husband. Just being around him during my summer vacations opened a world of wisdom that came from a lifetime of his serving in the fauj. He'd teach, share and mentor with a generous heart anyone willing to learn. From laying the table properly, answering landline phones with etiquette, and reaching somewhere on time, the spirit of army life continued to flow from both my grandparents to their children, and then to us, the grandchildren.

While growing up, I was enamoured with his meticulous paperwork, consistent routine, balanced lifestyle, and focus on bringing quality into all aspects of life. I'd quietly notice how people from all walks of life looked up to him for advice and help of all kinds and he'd selflessly and resourcefully help them out. A visionary, he could spot opportunities as well as risks way ahead of the times. His booming voice commanded respect and admiration wherever he went. My favourite part was listening to stories of his childhood and when he joined the army, how the fauj turned a young, energetic, restless boy into an officer and a gentleman. Spiritual introspection evolved; he had a deep impact on my own ability to live life consciously and authentically. Nana was and remains my Hero.

My grandmother complimented and contrasted beautifully as a partner to my grandfather. As a child, I honestly believed my grandmother had some magic in her hands. How she'd churn out the most amazing things out of nothing was beyond me. From the quintessential fauji trunk turned into a cosy sitting corner to crocheting exquisite table covers and stoles, my loving Nani could do it all.

I'd savour the stories of how she, as a young army wife, learned to overcome the innumerable challenges of fauji life with sheer grit and resourcefulness. In her heydays, I loved how beautifully Nani carried herself- from her classic style of clothes to her handbags, she always stood out in a crowd of people.

Slowly as I was growing, I realised how many values of army life had percolated into our home and hearts too. I saw the same magical touch in my mother, the ability to transform any space into a warm and welcoming home with whatever resources or situations life threw at her. As young growing girls, my friends and I admired and emulated her regal dress sense, her courage in the face of whatever life brought up, and most of all her ability to live life fully.

In her, I saw my grandfather's impressive personality and my grandmother's heart-warming lifestyle. In the civilian environment that my brothers and I grew up in, we usually stood out for various reasons, many of which actually came from having a mother from a forces background. People would often compliment her on how confident we came across as, or how pleasantly we'd answer the phone. Today, when I reflect upon this, I realise how diversity, inclusion, and respect for elders were just woven into our basic fabric, thanks to our upbringing.

At this juncture of my life, where I am a mom to an amazing teen, I savour and share the most amazing stories of valour, courage and honour that have been passed on to us across several generations of being a part of the family called the army. I also hope to pass on some of the values and the wonderful spirit of it.

Often in challenging situations, I draw strength from the wonderful legacy that has been passed on to us. I ask myself— what would Nana-Nani do in this situation?

Sure enough, clarity emerges, and strength follows!

Vandana Parashar

Therapy

on autoplay the birdsong
morning ritual
I mimic koel mimics me

unexpected showers
every puddle sets free
the child in me

one-way street
the fragrance of jasmine
everywhere

evening tea
with every sip
the sun slips

rolling hills
the wobbly sun slips
from this tree to that

silent night
raindrops trick the roof
into conversation

nudging
each other out of my selfie
summer clouds

nippy night
how slowly your fingers
find mine

flushed cheeks
what am I
to a butterfly

weekend getaway
we bring back grass-scented
memories

It All Ends Well

every cloud laden
with the promise of rain
dating app

suave doctor
I toss the apple
in dustbin

back home
I save his number
"lesson learnt"

mature love
I dip my feet
before jumping in

matrimonial
can a libran balance
my shopping bags

wedding stage
papa holds my hand
before the groom does

pregnancy report
my dad's face flushed
with my happiness

daddy's princess
every morning his toe nails
painted red

pink moon
her little face smudged
with my lipstick

walnut shell...
what was my life before
my daughters were born

Vinita Narula

The Fauji Fun

When a proposal to marry came from the family friends of the previous three generations it was a clear cut straight forward "NO" from my side with a perfect reason as to who wants to marry a nomad who moves places, cities, towns, houses every two three years or even worse, every now and then. Being used to a permanent continuous stay of twenty-two years in the best central Delhi colony that was specifically allotted to the senior government employees called Pandara Road, which happened to be a couple of metres away from the iconic India Gate and may be two kilometres away from the prestigious Connaught Place.

I had been on the teaching faculty of the esteemed Lady Irwin College of the Delhi University since August of 1966 which too happened to be just about two and a half kilometres away and one walked this distance comfortably quite frequently, the mere thought of an army type nomadic living idea sounded foolish and therefore was rejected outright even without any further blink of the eye. Providence has its own plans that they say are predestined!! As luck would have it, the predestined ones became a reality pushing the ill designed to a back seat and matrimony did happen. Shifting towns, cities and residences became a norm at "Family and Non family stations". Professional permanent status of the self-meant taking classes of graduate and postgraduate students at college remained the same and would join dear Sudhir at the place of his posting during the term vacations and later school holidays once the children had arrived. As a result one permanent residence always remained in New Delhi and the second or third etc. wherever he moved as per his postings.

The year we got married, Sudhir was posted at the Western Command located at Shimla and our first house allotment was at Himland Hotel, the whole floor of which was leased to the army to be used as officer's family accommodation. Each residential unit consisted of two rooms, a bathroom, a tiny kitchenette and a narrow long common roofed veranda. Actually this habitat had a make shift arrangement in which one of the original hotel bathroom seats had been covered with a wooden enclosure to work as cooking counter by placing the gas burner and prepare meals on hahahaa….. whereas the second pot contraption kept serving the purpose it was meant to. The common open veranda faced a dense jungle which was inhabited by Flying foxes, Monkeys, Langoors and other such like wild creatures, giving an eternal feel of living in a sanctuary!!! Our stay in this house lasted only for a couple of months and we were allotted a proper two roomed house at a locality named "Brock Hurst" located in "Chotta Simla"

It was truly a very pretty little house just that one's car needed to be parked some three hundred metres away and one morning being alerted by the neighbourhood Samaritans that all the four tyres of the vehicle had been slashed by some drunken miscreants at night and the poor thing was lying on the ground on its belly in a zero-degree temperature. The other challenge encountered was that to reach the better locations of the hill town one needed to negotiate a ninety-degree incline or say just about !!! There were however many pluses too like the local goodies availability in the small market around actually makes one's mouth water till date, some of these unforgettable relishes being the freshly baked bread and buns, sweetmeats (mithais) loaded with sugar and thickened fresh milk, earlier unseen unheard-of fruits like small marble sized pink colour plums with blood red colour flesh around the stone and delicious cherry red peaches, wah wah and wah again.

The next heaven like abode allotted by the army for the family stay in was the second floor suite number 227-228 in the Clark's

Hotel, the small kitchenette of which faced the all famous Mall Road and the French window of one of the bedrooms actually saw the passerby enjoy the hill queen Shimla in all its glory, for me incidentally this was the spot where I thoroughly enjoyed the post-partum nourishment of delicious "home- made Panjiri" sent by dear mother with all her love and blessings and me extremely thankful to god for blessing us with our son in Himachal Pradesh, thereby making it possible to buy property in this hill state by virtue of him being a domicile by birth if and when he wished to. Although this was a distant dream yet it was an additional reason to feel happy about.

We were thrilled when Sudhir got his next posting as the AD regiment in Delhi Cantt. Being allotted T-8 Cassels Road, a Barracks accommodation meant having a lavish row of eight rooms, big and small along with five quarters at its back (within its boundary wall) plus a huge kitchen garden or one may even call it a farm, in between to grow wheat, water melons and all vegetables etc. sufficient for all the inhabitant families. Arrays of seasonal flowers next to the entry gate pleased everyone no end, including the passersby. The tilted keekar tree in the front is standing tall even today and is a testimony to our really happy times spent on its soil. This living space was listed as a temporary accommodation in the army records and therefore the family got promoted to live in a permanent one at 6, Tigris Road, incidentally with another slanting tree in the front and a HUGE kitchen garden at the back, which was sufficient to grow enough vegetables not only to meet the daily family needs but also enough to reach the college friends and colleagues on a day-to-day basis. Outside the boundary wall at the back was the parade ground to give pleasure and enthuse the children at home day in and day out, with many regular activities like the Band practice, Cricket matches and functions like marriages taking place. There was truly a fun galore. Station canteen some fifty metres away, artillery mess on the adjacent road, regiment at the end of the road meant the naughty children's broken noses and limbs could be attended to without even minutes delays. Army rations got replenished on a regular basis mostly before the previous lot had got exhausted, regiment manufactured colas were always available, Raising days and other regimental activities kept every one upright, smarts and ever well dressed, smiling and in the best of spirits etc.

But moving on to Meerut, Sudhir's next posting and not getting a family accommodation meant that the family had to make do by living only in brother officer's vacant houses when they had gone on leave or some other assignment etc. But it was smiles, guffaws and all through. All in all to sum up, I can plainly say that fauj has always given and continues to give what no other service can. It makes one feel like a royal king/ queen as also a pauper, a beggar but everything in good spirit, in the name of brotherhood and the country AND that is a lot of fun. I am also not sure if I indeed was being wise in taking such a long time to say yes to marry the army man Sudhir when the proposal initially had come from his family. To speak the truth and being honest, on the hind side I am ready to confess that had I not agreed I would have missed all the fauji fun of shifting into newer houses ever so frequently in comparison to living in the Pandara Road permanent one for over twenty-two years.

Vivek Kamthan

"Bound By Wings: Triumphs Of The Indian Aviators"

In this magnificent land, where dreams took flight,
Three comrades united, their future burning bright.
From DPS RK Puram, their roots were entwined,
Young hearts, eager souls, with dreams defined.

They were young and idealist, so eager to serve,
Always mocking danger, Oh! What a nerve!
Trio wanted to fly like birds, soaring high like poetry,
To fulfil their destiny, and touch the sky with glory.

Together, they joined NDA, determined to go,
Bound by a passion, a friendship to grow.
They grew as fighters, with eyes shining wide,
A brotherhood formed; chests swelled with pride.

At Air Force Academy, they soared on wings,
Learning the art of flight and the joy it brings.
In the sky's embrace, they found their true home,
Bound by destiny, through skies they roam.

One took to the fighter, sleek and fierce,
A jet-propelled stallion, striking to pierce.
In supersonic speeds, he danced with grace,

Unleashing his fury, that no one can trace.

For he was a fighter pilot, true, bold and brave,

With eyes like an eagle, determined to save.

He trained so hard, a warrior in the making,

His passion for the sky, there was no mistaking.

Oh! The fighter, a winged predator of the sky,

With afterburners ablaze, it smoothly fly-by.

Looks sleek and deadly, with missiles and guns,

In dogfights, it stings, until the enemy runs.

The second, a helicopter pilot, skilled in his craft,

He soared through the air, his spirit ever steadfast.

Through valleys and mountains, he'd gracefully glide,

With each rotor rotation, conquering the sky so wide.

A helicopter pilot with amazing skill,

A guardian of air, hovering with will.

Rotors spinning, a symphony of flight,

Rescuing souls, a beacon of hope in the night.

The helicopter, a saviour in the air,

Its blades slicing through, without any care.

Vertical take-offs, nimble and free,

Saving lives from danger, from hills to sea.

The third, a transport aircraft's loyal guide,

Shouldering burdens, with strength dignified.

A behemoth in flight, its wings extended,

Delivering hope, when everything else ended.

The transport aircraft, a mighty giant above,

Carrying troops and cargo, fuelled by love.
Across vast distances, it'd soar and glide,
A lifeline of nation, with valour and pride.
Transport aircraft pilot, was bold, strong and true,
Carrying soldiers and supplies, always duty he'd pursue.
But in times of war, he'd switch roles with ease,
Flying bombers, protecting the land and its peace.

As they embarked on their journeys diverse,
Each pilot faced trials; their souls immersed.
Then came the Kargil War, their destiny's call,
A battle for honour, one that would enthral all.

The transport pilot, his aircraft took fire,
Nursed it to safety, fuelled by inner desire.
With a wounded aircraft, he refused to give in,
To safety he steered, victory his kin.
He landed with scars, but his spirit unbroken,
A hero in the skies, his story outspoken
Through smoke and chaos, he emerged unscathed,
A hero's spirit, unyielding and unsheathed.
The fighter pilot, entrusted with a critical task,
In crucial Ops, his weapon systems failed, alas!
Embracing unyielding resolve, he charted his course,
To willingly sacrifice himself, to take out target with force.

He turned his aircraft into a deadly bomb,
A blazing comet, soaring with aplomb.

The enemy position met its demise,
But the fate of the pilot, hidden from eyes.

His buddy, the helicopter pilot, valiant and true,
Undertook SAR for his comrade, a mission he'd pursue.
Through treacherous terrain, and the incoming storm,
Heart full of hope, his spirit resilient, in true form.
In mortal danger was his friend, and the skies also wept,
Forgetting safety, raging guns and rockets, enemy he swept.
Triumphantly together, they soared on rotors of grace,
Bound in victory, leaving only mayhem to erase.
These magnificent men and their flying machines,
From NDA to AFA, where dreams ascend serene.
They took to the skies, their spirits ablaze,
A symphony of sacrifice, in motherland's praise.

Oh, fighter, helicopter and transport aircraft too,
You carried their dreams and hopes, through and through.
You were not merely machines, you were their guide,
Their wings, their freedom, their source of pride.

But unseen, a friend stood tall,
One engineer among them, answering the call.
Behind the scenes, his presence strong,
The unsung protagonist, can't afford to be wrong.
Amidst the flying heroes, he quietly strode,
Master of machines, in mesmerising abode.
In hangars and tarmac, his kingdom was found,

Breathing life into metal birds, with skills renowned.

Oh, the engineer, a silent hero indeed,
Whose contributions in mute, met every need.
He toiled behind the scenes, his spirit pure,
Supporting their missions, of that he was sure.

For in the realm of aviation, teamwork prevails,
Pilots and engineers, a bond that never fails.
Their synergy of skill, a symphony of might,
Together they conquered, in the realm of flight.

Through the Kargil War, their unity held true,
The engineer's dedication, an unfaltering value.
He worked through nights, to mend what was torn,
Repairing the machines, for battles yet unborn.

In the annals of valour, their stories shall be told,
The triumphant pilots, courageous and bold.
But let us remember, amidst their lofty flight,
The toiling engineer, a reassuring calming sight.

So here's to the engineer, a silent force, unseen,
Whose devotion and expertise, remain behind scene.
In the world of aviation, where innovation redeems,
Here's a hero, behind magnificent flying machines.
Through the skies, their journeys intertwined,
Pilots and Engineer, forever entwined.

In the motherland, their stories shall be sung,

Those magnificent men, who dared to dream young.

From school to academy, their journey profound,

A testament to friendship, their spirits unbound.

In the realm of Indian aviation, their legacy shall stay,

Guiding future aviators, along their destined way.

For they were the heroes, with wings made of gold,

Those magnificent men, whose stories here unfold.

हिन्दी

आर्या कुमारी
शहीदों को प्रणाम

जब-जब आता है शहीदों का नाम,

सर सबने गौरव से उठाया होगा,

क्या होता है उनकी गैरमौजूदगी में, ये दृश्य किसी ने ना दिखाया होगा,

किन किताबों में होगा उन वादों का जिक्र,

जो जंग पर जाने से पहले जवानो ने अपने परिवार से किया था,

किन शब्दों में किया जाएगा उन वीरांगनाओं का बयान,

जो महीनों पहले ब्याह कर घर आई थी,

वो कौन से अक्षर होंगे जो उस सैनिक की कहानी को लिखेंगे,

जिसने अपनी बच्ची को भी ना देखा था,

कौन सुनेगा उन बच्चों की किलकारियां जो उनके बहादुर शहीद पिता के लिए हैं,

ये वो वीर गाथाएँ हैं, जो शब्दों की मोहताज़ नहीं हैं,

ये गाथाएँ गूंजती हैं,

उन पहाड़ों में,

जहां कई वीरों की सांसें थम गई हैं,

जहां नदी का रंग लाल हुआ,

जहां दुश्मनों का हाल बेहाल हुआ,

जहां दुश्मनों ने पीठ दिखाई,

जहां भारत के वीरों ने सीने पर गोली खाई,

जहां ऑक्सीजन से ज्यादा शौर्य की गाथा है,

जहां शॉल कम और बर्फ़ की चादर ज्यादा है,

जहां पहाड़ की चोटियाँ कम और अदमय साहस ज्यादा है,

100 करोड़ घरो में दिए जलते रहे इसलिये 527 वीरो ने अपने घरो के दिये बुझा दिये,

भारत माँ के आँचल के लिये, घर बैठी माँ के आँचल कुर्बान किये,

ये लहू से लिपटा हुआ तिरंगा,

भारत का स्वाभिमान है,

भारत के वीर सैनिकों को भारत का प्रणाम है।

अभिषेक आनंद त्रिपाठी
विजय प्रयाण

भारत की महिमा का फिर से, हो स्वर्णिम गुणगान
हो जाग्रत चैतन्य राष्ट्र का, चल पड़े पुनः अभियान
अखिल विश्व कल्याण हेतु से, रथ यह गतिशील रहे
पुनः प्राकट्य हो कृष्ण का, गीता की फिर धार बहे

राम हमारे हृदय अरण में, आकर फिर एक बार बसें
सबके मन में बसे दशानन, को मुक्ति का दान करें
हम अतीत के गौरव से, फिर वर्तमान को साहस दें
विश्व गुरु के गौरव पद का आज पुनः सम्मान करें

हम भविष्य का मार्ग ढूंढने, न औरों का आनन देखें
बीज अभी भी पास हमारे, बस अपने आँगन में ढूंढे
निधियों का संसार छुपा, हम भाग रहें हैं खुद से ही
चपल तड़ित के हम प्रकाश में, भूले अपना पथ भी

इतिहास के पन्नों से ही, सूर्य भविष्य का उगता है
जब उगता दैदीप्य सूर्य, तब अंधकार धुल जाता है
वही सूर्य गतिशील हुआ, फिर दिव्य देह ले आया है
गत गौरव का गान किए, नव राष्ट्र बनाने आया है

वही अरुण हम सबके भीतर, उगने को व्याकुल है
दिव्य अंशु से अपने हमको, वह भरने को आतुर है
बस एक आहुति हवन कुंड में, हम सबको देना है
निज स्वार्थों का ग्रहण लगा जो उसको धो देना है

एक बार उसके अंदर से, अपने को एकाकार करें
भारत माँ के आँचल का, एक बार हम मान रखें
विश्व गगन में लहराने को, जो ध्वजा हमारी तत्पर है
उसके हेतु से हम अपने, तन मन धन का दान करें

रोम रोम से राम राम की ध्वनि से हम अभिभूत रहें
आने वाले कुरुक्षेत्र में हम योद्धा बनकर तैयार रहें
नए रूप में युद्ध पुरातन, हर काल खंड में होता है
जय के गीत वही लिखता जो इतिहास को जीता है

इतिहास की स्मृतियों में हम, एक बार फिर झांके
आने वाले कल की खातिर, हम बीते कल में ताकें
भारत का अभियान निरंतर, सतत प्रवाहित होगा
और सनातन भग भारत का चहुँ ओर प्रकाशित होगा

भारत माँ की जय की ध्वनि से, अम्बर डोल उठेगा
केसरी अपने गहन नींद से अब निश्चित जाग उठेगा
बस एक बार भोले शंकर को, हाँ रौद्र रूप धरना है

बस एक बार शक्ति को अबकी काली बने विचरना है

बस एक बार, बस एक बार, पांचजन्य बोल उठेगा
बस एक बार गांडीव पार्थ का, हाँ रण में टूट पड़ेगा
गदा भीम की प्यास बुझाने, को देखो मचल रही है
जिसने माँ के भेद किए, उन प्राणों को मांग रही है

मैंने भी अब धनुष हाथ ले खुद को साध लिया है
मस्तक पर आशीष विजय का माँ से मांग लिया है
आओ मेरे साथ चलो, विजय प्रयाण पर चलते हैं
इस वसुधा का कर्ज बचा जो, उसको आज चुकाते हैं

अभ्युदय प्रकाश
हे रघुनंदन तेरी जय हो।

कौशल्या के प्रियतम दुलारे,

दशरथ के आंखों के तारे,

लक्ष्मण, भरत, शत्रुघ्न के भ्राता प्यारे,

माँ सीता के प्रभु तुम तारनहारे।

करुँ वंदन हे रघुनंदन तेरी जय हो!

नेतृत्व कौशल की तूने अजय या ध्वजा लहराई,

तप त्याग समर्पण से इंसानियत की राह दिखाई,

हर संबंधों का निर्वहन करते नहीं नैतिकता से बोध कराई,

तेरे अवतार ने प्रभु हमें जीने की कला सिखाई।

करुँ वंदन, हे रघुनंदन तेरी जय हो!

राज्य छोड़ प्रभु अरण्यों का वास सुखद नहीं हुआ होगा?

सुख को त्याग, दुःख के साथ समय मुशिक बीता होगा।

पत्नी-वियोग भी हृदय को बेहद खला होगा।

लक्ष्मण को लगा शक्ति बाण, प्रभु सर्प दंश सा लगा होगा।

करुँ वंदन, हे रघुनंदन तेरी जय हो!

तेरे जीवन के सिद्धांत हमेशा जीवित रहेंगे।

अध्यात्म इन्सानियत और नैतिकता को सींचेंगे

सत्य को सुदृढ़ कर आत्मसंयम को समुचित बल देंगे।

लक्ष्योन्मुख हो, प्रबल प्रतिज्ञा कर आत्मविश्वास पल्लवित करेंगे।

करूँ वंदन, हे रघुनंदन तेरी जय हो!

प्रभु, किन शब्दों में करूँ गुणगान तेरी,

तेरे यश कीर्ति की नहीं बखान शक्ति मेरी,

टूटी-फूटी ज्ञान से करू विनती और फेरी,

बन जाऊँ प्रभु कृपापात्र आपका,

एकमात्र आकांक्षा मेरी।

दुःख एक जैविक अनुभूति

जैविक चेतना की जागृति का आधार,

ब्रह्मांड के सृजन एवं संचालन का भी भार,

हर युग, स्थान एवं प्राणी में भिन्न प्रकार,

रखते सब कोसों दूर, कोई न करता मुझको प्यार।

सत्य को प्रमाण झूठ पर करूँ प्रहार,

नैतिक सिद्धांतों को सींच बेईमानी पर भी मार,

आराम, सुख-सुविधा को त्याग कष्टों से प्यार अपार,

तन मन को झकझोर कर करूँ शक्ति का प्रसार।

पीढ़ियों को देखकर सीख करूँ ऊँचे संस्कार,

प्राकृतिक आपदाओं से दुर्घटनाओं तक मेरे असीमित आकार,

व्यक्तिगत से सामूहिक विनाशलीला दिखाकर करती अपना इज़हार

सृष्टि के संतुलन को ठीक कर करूँ ईश्वरीय विधान साकार।

सुख से खेले आँख मिचौली, मेरा संदेश यह बारंबार,

सुख होता क्षणिक, दुख में ही होता अक्सर संसार,

युद्ध, आर्थिक तंगी कभी कोरोना लाकर करती मैं वैश्विक श्रृंगार,

वास्तविकता से अवगत होकर ही जीवों में निखार।

मेरा इस दुनिया से बस एक विचार,

सुख कामना छोड़ मुझे आलिंगन करें हर बार,

मेरी अनुभूति ही है चरम सुख का द्वार,

मेरे हर रूप, गुण करें 'बेहतर कल' का आभार।

आदित्य देशमुख

मैं हूँ

हर शंख का हुंकार मैं हूँ,
शक्ति की दहाड़ मैं हूँ,
हिमालय शिखर से लेकर,
समुद्र की गहरायी मैं हूँ।

ललाट शंभु अर्थ मैं हूँ,
भूमिहीन व्यर्थ मैं हूँ,
शत्रु का संहार मैं हूँ,
पृथ्वी का शृंगार मैं हूँ।

शांति के रक्षार्थ मैं हूँ,
प्यार का परिहार मैं हूँ,

साधु सा तेजस्वी मैं हूँ,
क्रूरता का हल भी मैं हूँ।

नील नभ से प्रशांत हूँ,
मैं अदृश्य अंधकार हूँ,
सच का मैं प्रकाश हूँ,
ब्रह्मांड सा प्रचंड हूँ।

लांघ ना पाए मेरी शाखाएँ,
अजानुबाहु वृक्ष हूँ,
सौम्यता की परिभाषा,
सर्वोपरि नाश हूँ।

आदित्य पवार
मेहँदी के आँसू

फिर हवाओं में बेरुख़ी सी है

सूनी आँखों में नमी सी है।

हथेलियों का खालीपन फिर उभर आया है

क्या फिर उसी सपने ने तुझे नींद से जगाया है।

आखिर कब तक दोष

अपने ही माथे मढ़गी

अपनी सूनी कलाइयों की वजह

खुद को कब तक कहोगी

माथे पर सिंदूर, नही सुहाता तुम्हें

पर ये बता, आखिर रंगों से भला कब तक लड़ोगी।

हाँ जानता हूं उसका वादा अधूरा रह गया

तेरे संग जन्मों का नाता कच्चा रह गया।

पर उसकी यादों के समुंदर में डूब-भर जाना आसान है

उससे उबरना, हालातों से लड़ने में ही असली मुक़ाम है।

तेरे अंदर उसे लौ बन कर जलने दे

खुद को अंधेरों से निकलने की आदत पड़ने दे।

उसे तेरी मायूसियों की वजह मत बना

वो हर खुशी था तेरी,

उसे अपने होठों की हसीं बनने दे

अब उसके हिस्से की जिम्मेदारियों को

अपने कंधों पर सजने दे।

श्रद्धांजलि : श्री बिपिन रावत

वक़्त का पहिया भी कमाल करता है
उगते सूरज को भी शाम करता है
कामयाबियों ने जिनके कदमों को चूमा
उन्हीं के आशियाँ को वीरान करता है।

वक़्त का पहिया भी कमाल करता है।
कंधों पर सजाये देश भर की उम्मीदें
छाती पर साहस की गाथायें समाई
जिनके होने से रोशन थी वीरों की दुनिया
उनके अपनों कि दुनिया क्यों उजड़ी- लड़खड़ाई।

वक़्त का पहिया भी कमाल करता है
उगते सूरज को भी शाम करता है।

आकांक्षा मोदानी
मैं 'नारी'

कहकशां है ये ज़िन्दगी,

छोड़ देती है पदचिन्ह।

गहरे पर मटमैले से,

समय के बहाव में बहते हुए,

मुश्किलों के भंवर से गुजरते हुए,

आलम बहाव का है,

या

टकराव उस शिला का,

क्या पल गिनेंगे उस आगाज़ को?

सफरनामें का साथ निभाने में....

क्या समझेंगे योगदान इसका....

या

गिला रखेंगें गर न कर पाए,

जीवन में किसी के उजाला।

संघर्ष खुद से स्वयं का,

क्या कीमत नहीं होती?

ज़िन्दगी सिर्फ मेरी कीमती क्यों नहीं होती।

अक्स मेरा वजूद किसी और का, स्वीकार नहीं मुझे!

समझौता हर बार दरकार नहीं मुझे।

देखो! ममत्व ने ठहरा दिया …

कर दिया मेरा विस्तार,

पदचाप आयी है हौले से,

करा गयी नारी को स्वीकार।

सक्षमता में वर्चस्व है तेरा,

पुरुषत्व हिला न पायेगा,

ओतप्रोत है तू ममता से,

वजूद तो उसमें भी निखर आएगा।

अखिलेश यादव
'शीलम्-परम-भूषणम्'

राजस्थान के धौलपुर का राष्ट्रीय मिलिट्री स्कूल, मेरे जीवन के लिए विद्यालय होकर भी किसी विश्वविद्यालय से कम नहीं रहा। वहाँ जो शिक्षा मिली वो बस किताबी नहीं बल्कि ताउम्र काम आनेवाली सच्ची सीख रही। 'शीलम्-परम-भूषणम्' मतलब 'Character is the Highest Virtue' जैसे आदर्श वाक्य की सीख आज भी मेरे लिए प्रकाश स्तंभ की तरह है। राष्ट्र से प्रेम और उसके लिए जीवन को लगा देने की प्रेरणा वहीं से मिली।

1983 से 1989 तक, क्लास 6 से 12 तक वहाँ मानसिक क्षमताओं के साथ-साथ मेरी शारीरिक क्षमताओं का भी विकास हुआ और दैनिक अनुशासन का भी। वहाँ का कठिन जीवन दरअसल आज राजनीति में काम आ रहा है। भोर में उठना, पीटी करना, तैयार होकर, नाश्ता करके कई किमी चलकर स्कूल आना-जाना वो भी राजस्थान की गर्मी में; पढ़ना, खेलना-कूदना, हर तरह के स्पोर्ट्स में नियमित रूप से भाग लेना; ये कठिन जीवन सही मायनों में हमें हमारे आनेवाले कल के लिए तैयार कर रहा था। धूल-पसीने से कभी न घबराना और चौबीसों घंटे लगातार काम करने की ताक़त रखना, ये भी तो एक सीख ही थी।

मुझे लगता है राष्ट्रीय मिलिट्री स्कूल में पढ़ा हुआ कोई भी बच्चा कभी भी किसी से न तो डरता है, न दबता है। संघर्ष और चुनौतियों से उसकी शक्ति दोगुनी-चौगुनी होती है। वो तपे हुए लोहे के समान होता है और सबसे बड़ी बात वो विपरीत-से-विपरीत परिस्थितियों में भी हमेशा सकारात्मक होता है, पॉज़िटिव रहता है। मैं आज जो भी हूँ, वो वहाँ के उन गुरुजनों की वजह से हूँ जिन्होंने मुझे संवारा और हमेशा बेख़ौफ़ होकर सबके हक़ की लड़ाई ईमानदारी से लड़ने के लिए तैयार किया और ये भी सिखाया कि बड़ी सोच और बड़े लक्ष्यों से निर्देशित और ग़रीब, शोषित व किसी ज़रूरतमंद की सच्चे मन से मदद करनेवाली एक सौहार्दपूर्ण और नेक ज़िंदगी जीने से ही जीवन सार्थक होता है। मैं उन सबका आभारी भी हूँ और सच्चे मन से कृतज्ञ भी।

प्रज्ञा बाजपेयी द्वारा साक्षात्कार

धौलपुर का राष्ट्रीय मिलिट्री स्कूल में परेड करते अखिलेश यादव

अनीता शर्मा
अश्क़

बहुत मसरफ़ के हैं
खामोश से अश्क़
यह दिल और दृष्टि
दोनों की धूल बहा देते हैं

कभी अजनबी बन कर
पलकों में चुभने लगते हैं
और कभी पिघल कर
ख़ुद मलहम बन जाते हैं

रंजिशों का सैलाब हो
या फिर खुशी की इंतिहा

मैंने दोनो की सरहद पर
इन बेपनाह बूंदों को पाया है

वात्सल्य की बसंत हो
या फिर विरह की शरद
चिलमनों के गलियारे में
हर मौसम में घिर आते हैं

हल्का है इनका वजूद, फिर भी
बिन बुलाए मेहमान से आकार
धीमे से किसी औट से निकल कर
मन के बोझ को हल्का कर जाते हैं।

इंतजार

रात भर घर की छत पर
मैं और मेरा अज़ीज़
ये सौम्य, स्याह अम्बर
धैर्य के धागे से एकबद्ध होकर
करते रहे इंतजार.....

नहीं था चांद वहां गगन में
और ना जुगनू कोई ज़मीन पर
उसके विराने में ना एक सितारा
न कोई चिराग मेरे आँचल में
जो दे जाए कतरा रोशनी का

वहाँ थी तो बस सर्द हवा
यहाँ सिर्फ गहरा धुआं
और हम दोनों के बीच

सन्नाटे के फासले को टटोलते
सैंकड़ों अनकहे सवाल

उसके दामन में मोती ओस के
मेरी आंखों में लरजते असीम आंसू
दूर क्षितिज पर टकटकी बांधे
मैं और मेरा ख़ामोश हमसाया
बांटते रहे कई मौन पल

शायद दोनों को था इंतजार
बादलों को भेदती हुई
उस उज्जलि आरुशी का
जो दे जाए दोनों को यकीन
आने वाली रोशन सुबह का।

डी वी संतोष मेहेर
घर अस्थायी, यादें स्थायी

अभी कुछ दिनों पहले हमें
अपना घर बदलना पड़ा
ज़िन्दगी आगे बढ़ती रहे,
सो वक्त के साथ चलना पड़ा।

इसी घर में हमने अपने
कई हसीन पल गुज़ारे थे
उन पलों में कुछ मामूली थे
तो कुछ बेहद ख़ास और प्यारे थे।

माना की उस घर में कुछ
अनचाहे पल भी थे
मगर वो सारे पल भी
प्यार की आग़ोश में बीते।

कई हसीन पलों को समेटकर हम
अपने नए घर की ओर चल पड़े
कुछ और नई यादों के
नए महल बनाने को निकल पड़े।

कुछ दिन बाद वहाँ लौटकर गए तो
रिश्तों की मजबूती को मान लिया
जब गली के उन कुत्तों ने हमें
दुम हिलाते हुए पहचान लिया।

जब उस खाली घर में घुसे
तो देखा कि कई यादें बिखरी पड़ी थीं
उनमे कुछ यादें छोटी सी थीं
और कुछ यादें बहुत बड़ी थीं।

ऐसा लगा कि वो हवाएँ
कुछ मायूसी से महक रही थीं
वो बेरंग सी दीवारें हमारी
नामौजूदगी में सिसक रही थीं।

वो बाग जो खिलाया था हमने
वो अब लग रही थी वीरान सी
वो कलियाँ सारी ज़िन्दा तो थीं
पर हो गयी थीं बेजान सी।

बिन हमारे शायद उनकी भी खुशियों पे
निराशा अपनी परछाई फैला गयी
देखकर हमें खिल उठा वो माहौल सारा
और ख़ुशी की एक लहर सी छा गयी।

मुझे पता है कुछ ही दिनों में
उस घर में नए लोग आएंगे
इन मुरझाई हुई फ़िज़ाओं में
एक नयी ऊर्जा जगायेंगे।

ये बाग़ नए लोगों को देखकर
फिर से मुस्कुराके खिल जायेगा
इन हवाओं को अपना रंग बिखेरने का
एक नया मकसद मिल जायेगा।

ये दीवारें ये हवाएँ तो
शायद हमें भूल जायेंगी
पर इनके बीच गुजरी घड़ियाँ
हर लम्हा साथ निभायेंगी।

यूँ मकानों को घर बनाकर
निकल जाना हमारी मजबूरी है
क्योंकि अपने हालात के वश में रहकर
नई मंज़िल की ओर जाना ज़रूरी है।

चलो, अपने ज़िन्दगी के इस
दौर-ए-तरीके में खो जाते हैं
अपने नए घर में नयी उम्मीदों को
फिर नए सिरे से सजाते हैं।

गौतम नांद्रेकर
तस्वीर

उड़ान भरी उसने, नीले नभ की ओर

तरद्दुद मे, पलके बीना झपकाए देखता रहा

खींची गयी तस्वीरें तेरी

काश मै भी उड़ पाता, यही सोचता रहा।

कभी बादलों मे रहा गुम

कभी पहाड़ों के बीच

तो कभी नदियों को तु चूम

कलाबाजियां करता तु मस्त मगन

यही करना था तुझे

की तुमने मेहनत, लगायी अपनी पूरी लगन

जान कर भी अंजान रहे दोनो हम

तु चला चीरता गगन

देखो चल उड़ा हमारा रतन

तेरे घर वापसी की दुआऐ मांगी हर बार

दिखा तु रनवे (runway) के उस पारा।

थक गई नजरें मेरी राह देखते

जब कभी भी लौटा तु देर से बेस (Base)

पर खुश हुआ मै,

जब आया तेरा संदेश आय एम सेफ (I am safe)

बस अब तेरी यादें ही बची हैं

रह गई अपनी मुलाकात अधूरी है

तेरी मंजिल थी आसमान को छुना शान से

नन्हा परिंदा था, चला आस्मा की बांहो मे

तस्वीरे खींची मैंने बहुत

बस तस्वीरें ही खींचता रह गया मैं।

गोपाल पुरधानी

1.

पैदा हुआ जो इस मिट्टी से, वो हिन्द का कर्ज़दार हो गया।

और इसी पुख़्ता सबूत से, वो मेरा भी रिश्तेदार हो गया।

अलग अलग जाति धर्म में हम सब पैदा हुए;

यह देश अच्छे लोगों का, संयुक्त परिवार हो गया।

2.

खुदा की रहमतों की कोई इन्तहा ही नहीं।

उस की दया से तो कोई भी बचा ही नहीं।

गुनाहगार है तो उस के कदमों में गिर जा;

पनाहगिर की तो वहां कोई सज़ा ही नहीं।

3.

आसान जिंदगी की हर डगर नहीं होती।

कुछ रातों की तो जल्दी सहर नहीं होती।

यह तो सवाल हैं जो अक्सर उभर आते हैं;

दरअसल जवाबों की कोई उमर नहीं होती।

हरीश जोशी
बस कोई भूखा ना सोए आज

एक ऐसी पहल करें, कि एक दूसरे के काम आएं हम।

मानव को बचाने की जिम्मेदारी, अपने कंधों पर उठाएं हम।

क्या पाया, क्या गवाया, क्या कमाया, सब भूल जाएं हम।

बस कोई भूखा ना सोए आज, ऐसा कुछ कर जाएं हम।

वक्त है कि एहसान एक दूसरे पर करें और भूल जाएं हम।

किसी अनजान के दु:ख में, भागीदार बन जाएं हम।

कोशिश इतनी सी, कि किसी मानव के काम आ जाएं हम।

बस कोई भूखा ना सोए आज, ऐसा कुछ कर जाएं हम।

हर घर में हो खुशहाली, उद्देश्य ही अपना बनाएं हम।

होगा फिर एक नया सवेरा, उसकी उम्मीद दिलाएं हम।

चलो किसी गरीब की, भूख मिटा कर उसे अमीर बनाएं हम।

बस कोई भूखा ना सोए आज, ऐसा कुछ कर जाएं हम।

दूर है सरकार का रैन बसेरा, यह भी जानते हैं हम।

राहत पहुंचेगी जरूर पर, कुछ देर से समझते हैं हम।

चलो सब को जानकर, अनजान की मदद को निकले हम।

बस कोई भूखा ना सोए आज, ऐसा कुछ कर जाएं हम।

मां बाप भाई बहन, या कोई रिश्तेदार बन जाएं हम।

वह है मेरा, जो है भूखा, इतना पहचान जाएं हम।

हर रिश्ते से बड़ा मानवता का रिश्ता, यह भी जान जाएं हम।

बस कोई भूखा ना सोए आज, ऐसा कुछ कर जाएं हम।

सोचा है हमने जो कुछ, विश्वास उसी पर करते जाएं हम।

प्रार्थना हर मनुष्य के लिए, दिन रात करते जाएं हम।

चलो आज किसी भूखे के लिए, भगवान बन जाएं हम।

बस कोई भूखा ना सोए आज, ऐसा कुछ कर जाएं हम।

इन्दु तोमर

डोर मेरे दिल की तुम न कहीं और छोड़ आना

हर रोज़ की तरह

तुम जल्दी वापस आना

मैं सजा कर रखूँ

तुम्हारा पसंद का खाना

बस इतनी सी बात

बिन कहे समझ पाना

डोर मेरे दिल की तुम

न कहीं और छोड़ आना।

बंधन ये प्यारा मुझे है लुभाता

इसे घड़ी घड़ी सजाना

हक़ीक़त है मेरी जिंदगी

न इसे एक स्वप्न बनाना

कर्मपथ पर तुम चाहे

किसी भी तूफ़ान से टकराना

जब चेहरा याद आये मेरा

तो वापस यहीं चले आना।

डोर मेरे दिल की तुम

न कहीं और छोड़ आना

अमृत कड़वा ही सही पर

तेरे नाम का हर सुबह पिलाना

तू सरहद पर सही तेरी खुशबु से

मुझे हर शाम महकाना

तू शांत सिपाही सही मगर

तेरी वर्दी को हर रोज़ चमकाना

बस एक झलक तेरी तिरछी सी

और तू मंद मंद मुस्काना

डोर मेरे दिल की तुम

न कहीं और छोड़ आना

ये मैडल ये सितारे तेरी वर्दी की

शान है, सब को जरा बताना

जंग में घायल तो कभी

शांति दूत हो ये भी समझाना

वतनपरस्ती की ज़िद में आता

बखूबी तुम्हें शहीद हो जाना

बस काजल चूड़ी बिना बिंदिया के
औरत कैसे जाने सज पाना।
डोर मेरे दिल की तुम न

कहीं और छोड़ आना
बस साँझ ढले और तुम चले आना
तुम चले आना।।

इंदु वशिष्ठ
मोह मुक्ति

हम संसार में क्यों आए? हजारों बार यह प्रश्न हम सबके ज़ेहन में यदा-कदा आता है। जीवन के प्रारंभ में एक नन्हा शिशु अपनी किलकारियों की खुशियों से स्वयं प्रसन्न होता है और अपने इर्द-गिर्द सभी को खुशी देता है, विशेषकर अपने माता-पिता को, मानो उसकी दुनिया उन्हीं में सिमट गई है। बड़ा होते-होते धीरे-धीरे उसका दायरा अंतर्मुखी होने लगता है। दूसरों से स्वयं पर केंद्रित हो जाता है। परंतु अभी वह अपनी भौतिक आवश्यकताओं के लिए अपनों पर आश्रित होता है, समय के साथ-साथ उसकी सोच और दुनिया सीमित होने लगती है, और अपनों के लिए संकुचित। प्रायः यही कहते हैं कि ऐसा होना स्वाभाविक है, परंतु यह स्वाभाविकता अपने माता-पिता के लिए धीरे-धीरे एक ऐसा शून्य उत्पन्न कर देती है कि वह इसको या तो समझते नहीं या समझने का प्रयास ही नहीं करते। इस रिक्तता से माता-पिता में खालीपन और खोखलापन आने लगता है। शायद वह निशब्द हो जाते हैं तथा रिश्तो का एक आडंबर ओढ़ लेते हैं। ऐसा लगता है मानो बर्फ की चादर में उनका अस्तित्व बिल्कुल सिमट सा जाता है। मुझे कभी-कभी इससे बहुत पीड़ा और वेदना होती है परंतु ऐसा लगता है कि हम अपनी विवशताओं और स्वार्थ में इतना खो जाते हैं कि उनके इस मौन दर्द को महसूस ही नहीं कर पाते। वह समय भी आता है जब वह हमसे बिछड़ जाते हैं, और धीरे-धीरे स्वयं को उनकी जगह पर पाते हैं। फिर हम भी समय चक्र के साथ आगे बढ़ते हुए उसी ही कालखंड में पहुंच जाते हैं और जब माता-पिता को पीड़ा का जो एहसास होता है वही सत्य का आईना है। जीवन में इस चक्र का क्या अभिप्राय है जब तक हम समझ पाते हैं अवसान का समय निकट आ जाता है। क्या यही जीवन है बस इसकी पीड़ा को नहीं समझ पाते, शायद कोई भी नहीं। इसलिए यदि हम इस मौके बंधन में कर्म के साथ-साथ निर्लिप्त भी हो जाएं, शीघ्र ही इस पीड़ा और वास्तविकता को समझ जाएंगे। ऐसा करने के लिए आत्मज्ञान बहुत आवश्यक है तभी इन संबंधों की बेड़ियों से मुक्त होकर हम स्वतंत्र पंछी की तरह उन्मुख हो सकते हैं। काश समय पर समझ पाते पर ऐसा होता नहीं है, यही तो माया का चक्र चक्र है।

जितेन्द्र सिंह
शिंजर देखना होगा

मनाओ ईद तुम, आज मैं मातम मनाता हूँ

मरे हैं आज फिर कुछ लोग, चलो मैं दुःख जताता हूँ

मगर बच्चे जो बिकते थे, शिंजर के बाज़ारों में

जहाँ मासूम कटे उधड़े, बिखरे थे हज़ारों में

इतना ज़ुल्म बच्चों पर, क्यों तुमने चुप सहा बोलो

वो काफ़िर है क़तल कर दो, ये मैंने कब कहा बोलो

वो पेनी धार का ख़ंजर, वो ख़ंजर देखना होगा

अगर खून है, उबलता है, तो शिंजर देखना होगा

ख़लीफ़ा वो जो बन बैठा, खिलाफत की सज़ा मानो

उसे क्यों मुर्तज़ा माना, इसे भी मुर्तज़ा मानो

मैं तड़पा हूँ, ख़ुदा हूँ मैं, ख़ुदा राज़ी नहीं होगा

अभी लेह परस्ती से, कोई हाजी नहीं होगा

वो मंज़र देख तुम चुप थे, ये मंज़र देखना होगा

अगर मक्का रुलाती है, तो शिंजर देखना होगा

ममता पंडित
खनक

हंसती खिलखिलाती
ठहाके लगाती हुई औरतें
चुभती हैं तुम्हारी आँखों में
कंकड़ की तरह...
क्योंकि तुम्हें आदत है
सभ्यता के दायरों
में बंधी दबी सहमी
संयमित आवाज़ों की...

उनकी उन्मुक्त हँसी
विचलित करती है तुम्हें
तुम घबरा के बंद करने लगते हो
दरवाज़े खिड़कियां...
रोकने चलो हो उसे
जो उपजी है
इन्हीं दायरों के दरमियां।

कितने नादान हो की
जानते भी नहीं
की लांघ कर तुम्हारी सारी
लक्ष्मण रेखाओं को...
ध्वस्त कर तुम्हारे अहं की लंका
कब से घुल चुका है
वो उल्लास इन हवाओं में।

पहुँच चुकी है 'खनक'
हर उदास कोने में
जगाने फिर एक उम्मीद
उगाने थोड़ी और हंसी।

और हां तुम्हारी आँख का वो पत्थर
अब और चुभ रहा होगा।

मेरी दुआ

तुम सब जब युद्ध के शंखनाद से गर्वित हो,
मेरे माथे पर चिंता की रेखाएं उभर आयी हैं।
बहुत कोशिश है कि स्थिर दिखूँ,
पर आँखों में आशंकाएं उतर आयी हैं।

हो सकता है जग मुझे स्वार्थी समझे,
किंतु मैंने जो देखे है, वो घाव बहुत गहरे हैं।
जंग, जीत और जश्न तुम्हे मुबारक,
सामने मेरे बस मासूमों के चेहरे हैं।

शक मुझे ज़रा नहीं उनके पौरुष पर,
वो विजय वरण कर ही आएंगे।
सच है यह भी लेकिन, गर एक भी छूटा,
हम जश्न नहीं मना पाएंगे।

चाहे तुम मुझे कायर कहना,
मैं फिर भी शांति की दुआ मांगूंगी।
जब तक नहीं लौटते सकुशल सभी,
मैं उस अंतिम प्रहर तक जागूँगी।

नित्या शुक्ला
भोर का सपना

"तुमने यही किताब पढ़ने के लिए क्यों चुनी?"

"अरे! हर बात की कोई ना कोई वजह होती है।

शायद मुझे इस किताब का कवर पसंद आ गया,

या इस किताब की नायिका का नाम पसंद आया हो,

या फिर, हो सकता है कि मैं इसके लेखक को पसंद करता हूं,

इसलिए मैंने यह किताब चुनी।"

"हां सही कहा तुमने,

हर बात की कोई ना कोई वजह जरुर होती है।"

"चिड़ियों का चहचहाना,

सूरज का होना,

फूलों का खिलना,

बादलों का टकरा जाना,

बारिश का आना,

हवाओं का बहना,

गिरते आंसू,

मुस्कुराते होंठ,

हर बात की कोई ना कोई वजह होती है।"

"और प्यार"

"प्यार क्या?"

“प्यार होने की भी क्या कोई वजह होती है”

“पता नहीं”

“पर बेवजह, बेमतलब, निस्वार्थ, जुड़ा हुआ बंधन ही शायद प्यार है”

“हम्म्म शायद”

“आओ ना, हम तुम बेसबब, बेवजह, बेपनाह इश्क करें”

“चलो हटो, इश्क कोई काम है क्या”?

दूर कहीं से गाने की आवाज आई

“हमने देखी है इन आँखों की महकती खुशबू

हाथ से छू के इसे रिश्तों का इल्जाम न दो”

फिर आई ज़ोरदार आवाज़ “बूम”

और सब कुछ लाल हो गया।

ईशा घबराकर गहरी नींद से उठ बैठी।

सीने पर रखी किताब बंद कर, ईशा ने अपने गालों के गुलाबी रंग, चिंता के काले बादलों और सारे बुरे ख्यालों को जूड़े से बांधा और बेमन से गैस पर चाय चढ़ा दी।

आज रेडियो चालू नहीं किया शायद इसलिए कि कहीं रेडियो की आवाज़ में फोन की घंटी की आवाज ना गुम हो जाए।

फोन की घंटी जब पिछले हफ्ते बजी थी तब कबीर ने यही कहा था कि इस बार भी दिवाली पर छुट्टी मिलना मुश्किल है।

और ईशा अपना गुस्सा छुपाते हुए बोली थी “कोई बात नहीं मेजर साहब Nation First हमारा क्या है,

करवा चौथ पर फोटो देख व्रत तोड़ा तो दिवाली भी फोटो के साथ मना लेंगे।”

कबीर और ईशा दोनों ने अपनी टीस छिपा दस्तूर निभाते हुए फीका सा “आई लव यू” बोल फोन रख दिया था।

बस तभी से इस मुई फोन की घंटी ने मौन व्रत धारण कर लिया था। हाथों में चाय का कप पकड़े वह समाचार देखने लगी।

मन में यह दुआ लिए कि कहीं बारामुला लिखा हुआ ना दिखे ईशा सिर्फ नीचे फ्लैश हो रहे समाचार पढ़ रही थी।

तभी डोर बेल बजी समाचारों पर नज़रें गड़ाये ईशा खीझते हुए दरवाजे की तरफ बढ़ी

"चैन से सुबह की चाय भी नहीं पी सकती इतनी सवेरे कौन आ धमका?"

दरवाजा खोलते ही कबीर को सामने देख उसके हाथों से रिमोट और आँखों से खारे पानी का झरना गिर पड़ा।

कबीर ईशा को गले लगा कर शरारती मुस्कान के साथ बोला आ गया तुम्हारी आँखों में सावन और गाने लगा

"मोहब्बत बरसा देना तू सावन आया है"

आओ हम तुम बेसबब, बेहिसाब, बेइंतहा प्यार करें।

ईशा भोर का सपना याद कर

गुलाबी गालों और शरारती आँखों के साथ खिलखिलाने लगी।

दिवाली अब सच में दिवाली थी।

पियूष शर्मा
रजवाड़ टाइगर

मैं जो कहानी आपको सुनाने जा रहा हूं, ये कहानी बताती है कि कैसे इस देश के साधारण मध्यवर्गीय परिवार के बच्चे मेहनत करते हैं, अपने लक्ष्य को प्राप्त करने के लिए, देश सेवा के लिए, अपने सपनों को साकार करने के लिए।

यह वह कहानी है जिसे आप अपने परिवार में लोगों को बताना चाहेंगे, वह कहानी है जो कभी आपकी आंखों को नम करेगी तो कभी आपको अपने लक्ष्य की तरफ ले चलने में मदद करेगी।

आशुतोष के जीवन की कहानी एक साधारण मध्यवर्गीय परिवार के एक महत्वाकांक्षी बच्चे की कहानी है जो अपने दिल में देश सेवा का ज़ज्बा रखता था। बहुत इच्छा थी मां भारती के लिए कुछ कर गुजरने की पर कहते हैं कि पहले जिंदगी आपका इम्तिहान लेती है और फिर आप को सलाम करती है।

ईश्वर जब कोई बड़ी जिम्मेदारी देने की सोचता है तो पहले परखता है क्या आप उस जिम्मेदारी लेने के लिए बने हो कि नहीं तो? आशुतोष को भी बहुत सारी चुनौतियों का सामना करना पड़ा और उसके बाद एक "व्यक्ति से व्यक्तित्व" बनने की कहानी है आशुतोष की।

आशु से "रजवाड़ टाइगर" का सफर चुनौती पूर्ण और बहुत ही प्रेरणादायक है।

अगर कोई व्यक्ति अपने लक्ष्य को 2-3 बार में नहीं प्राप्त कर पाता तो वह उसको छोड़कर आगे बढ़ जाता है यह सोच कर कि मैं इसके लिए नहीं बना हूं। पर कुछ अपनी धुन के पक्के होते हैं और वह लगातार प्रयास करते रहते हैं जब तक कि जो मन में ठाना है वह नहीं मिल जाता और ऐसे ही थे कर्नल आशुतोष शर्मा।

आपको जानकर हैरानी होगी की लगातार 12 बार आर्मी के इंटरव्यू में रिजेक्ट होने के बाद भी कर्नल आशुतोष शर्मा अपने लक्ष्य से नहीं भटके, 13वे और अंतिम अटेम्प्ट में सेलेक्ट हुए, ऐसा ज़ज्बा था उसको आर्मी में जाने का।

तो कभी आप अपने लक्ष्य को लेकर निराश हो तो जरूर एक बार आशु को ध्यान कर लीजिएगा। छ: साल तक लगातार रिजेक्ट होने के बाद उसका सिलेक्शन हुआ।

मुझे आज भी ध्यान है उसका इंटरव्यू से रिजेक्ट होने के बाद जर्नल क्लास के डिब्बे के टॉयलेट के पास बैठ कर आना और जब मैं उसे लेने रेलवे स्टेशन जाता था तो मुझसे गले लग कर रोना और बस यही कहना भैया तुम मुझ पर भरोसा रखो मैं एक दिन सेलेक्ट हो कर दिखाऊंगा और तुम सबका नाम ऊंचा करूंगा। देश के लिए बड़ा काम करूंगा।

और फिर वो दिन आया जब आशू का आखिरी अटेम्प्ट में सिलेक्शन हुआ।

आर्मी ट्रेनिंग के बाद कर्नल आशुतोष शर्मा का चयन "ब्रिगेड ऑफ दी गार्ड्स" यूनिट में हुआ।

कर्नल आशुतोष आर्मी के उन चुनिंदा आर्मी ऑफिसर्स में से एक हैं जिन्हें तीन वीरता पदकों से सम्मानित किया गया।

एक सेना मेडल उन्हें तब दिया गया जब उन्होंने अपने एक जवान को बचाने के लिए आमने सामने की लड़ाई में एक आतंकवादी को मारा। कर्नल आशुतोष वीरता, देश भक्ति के साथ-साथ अपने जवानों और ऑफिसर्स से प्यार के लिए जाने जाते हैं।

2 मई 2020 की दोपहर को खबर मिली कि कुछ आतंकवादियों ने पांच कश्मीरी लोगों को बंदी बना लिया है, कर्नल आशुतोष बिना समय गवाएं अपनी टुकड़ी के साथ उसी स्थान पर पहुंचे। एक मुठभेड़ के बाद कर्नल आशुतोष और उनकी टीम ने बड़ी वीरता से लड़ते हुए उन पांचों भारतीय नागरिकों को सुरक्षित बचा लिया। नागरिकों को बचाते हुए एवं आतंकवादियों का निर्भरता पूर्वक मुकाबला करते हुए कर्नल आशुतोष को आतंकवादियों की गोली लगी और वह बहादुरी के साथ आतंकवादियों से मुकाबला करते हुए देश के लिए शहीद हो गए।

इस मुकाबले में कर्नल आशुतोष के साथ उनके चार साथियों ने भी अपनी जान गवांई।

"मेरी हिम्मत को परखने की गुस्ताखी न करना, पहले भी कई तूफानों का रुख मोड़ चुका हूं"..... यह लाइन कोई शायरी नहीं बल्कि कर्नल आशुतोष शर्मा का आखिरी व्हाट्सएप स्टेटस है।

उसने जिंदगी में कभी हार नहीं मानी ना तो जब जिंदगी उसका इम्तिहान ले रही थी, बार-बार इंटरव्यू में रिजेक्ट करके और ना ही देश के दुश्मनों से मुकाबला करते हुए।

आज भी पूरा देश कर्नल आशुतोष शर्मा के ज़ज़्बे को सलाम करता है। उनका नाम बड़े सम्मान के साथ दिल्ली के नेशनल वॉर मेमोरियल लिखा गया है।

कर्नल आशुतोष की कहानी आने वाली पीढ़ियों को कभी नहीं हिम्मत हारने की व अपने लक्ष्य जब तक सफलता न मिले तब तक उस की तरफ निरंतर प्रयास जारी रखने की शिक्षा देती रहेगी।

प्रज्ञा बाजपेयी
चल आज घर जल्दी चलते हैं

चल आज घर जल्दी चलते हैं
ओवर टाइम तो अक्सर करते हैं
आज सही समय पर निकलते हैं
आज किसी और से नहीं, वक़्त से
अपने लिये जंग लड़ते हैं...

चल आज बेवजह निकलते हैं
घर के काम से नहीं
रूहानी शाम के नाम निकलते हैं
कुछ दिल्लगी, कुछ मनमर्ज़ी करते हैं

चल आज सारी रात जागते हैं
सुबह जल्दी नहीं, देर से उठते हैं
चल आज योग नहीं, सैर पर चलते हैं
कुछ नया, कुछ बेतुका करते हैं

चल ए सी से निकल, खुली हवा में चलते
हैं
कार से नहीं बाइक से चलते हैं
कुछ जिंदादिली करते हैं
बहुत दिन से किसी उधेड़ बुन में हूं
चल आज भूलने का नाटक करते हैं
थोड़ा टेंशन कम करते हैं

चल आज कुछ बेतुकी बात करते हैं
काम की नहीं
कुछ अपनी, कुछ तेरी बात करते हैं
चल आज कुछ अपने लिए करते हैं
चल आज थोड़ा मुस्कुरा लेते हैं
फ़ोन बंद करते हैं
चल मिल कर बात करते हैं

प्रवेश धायल
आज़ाद

जो बात मन में है,
सीना ठोक कर गर कह पा रहे हो
तो आज़ाद हो तुम

ना अपनों की शर्म, ना गैरों का है खौफ़
बस ज़मीर को अपने तुम जिता रहे हो
तो आज़ाद हो तुम

जाति, रंग और अंग से कोसों आगे
जो हर एक शख़्स में ब्रह्म पा रहे हो
तो आज़ाद हो तुम

घोट कर पिलाए गए राष्ट्रवाद से परे
अपने ज़हन में पली देशभक्ति को निभा रहे हो
तो आज़ाद हो तुम

आज सभी लहरा रहे हैं
कल गर सड़क, नाले, टायर से तिरंगा बचा रहे हो
तो इस वीर भारत के आज़ाद हो तुम...

असल

दिल है खूब जवां

पर किस्से जिसके पुराने हैं

यादें क्या होती हैं, जाओ उस से पूछो।

मुकम्मल इश्क़ की तलाश में

गुज़रे जिसके ज़माने हैं

आशिकी क्या होती है, जाओ उस से पूछो।

ईश्वर मेरा है,

और उसी तरह शायद अल्लाह है तेरा

वो जो कल भूखा सोया था

ठिकाना आज का भी है नहीं

क्या रोटी से बड़ा मज़हब कोई है?

जाओ उस से पूछो!

पूजा अत्री
तन्हाई

बेबस दिल की चीखें सुनते हैं, ये सन्नाटे रातों के,
अंधेरों के साए सताते हैं, हमें जानलेवा तन्हाइयों में।
बैठूं कभी मैं जब वीराने में, खुद मे खुद को ही ढूंढूं मैं,
मन के भीतर समेटे बैठी, अनकहे अल्फाज़ो को मैं,
लब पर आने को ये तरसे कब तक समेटूं इस तूफ़ाँ को मैं।

तन्हाई ने खामोश रातें चुनी,
इस दिल ने बस तेरी प्रीत की धुन सुनी,
है ये कैसी ख़लिश मन की,
क्यों मेरी ये दुनिया तुझ पर ही बस है थमी।

तरसती निगाह, मचलते अरमां और मेरी ये खामोश जुबां,
करे धड़कने हौले से कानों में सरगोशियां,
क्यों बीते ये सारा जीवन बन के कोरा कागज़,
डूबे तेरी प्रीत में ऐसे कि बन जाये अमर कहानियाँ।

कहने को है अनेकों रिश्ते, फिर भी रह जाते हम अधूरे,
सब की है इक अपनी मंज़िल,
हर कोई है मझधार में छोड़े,
रह जाती केवल तन्हाई,
इस अनोखे जीवन की बस यही है सच्चाई।

बारिश

आसमां को ज़मी से मिलने की

ख्वाहिश शाम ओ सहर,

निर्भीक बरसे ऐसे ये मेघ,

भर दे ज़मी का आंचल

कि पड़ा है कब से यूंही ये बंजर।

जब ज़िन्दगी की उलझनों का हो हम पे सितम,

सिसकता हुआ मन और आँखें हो ये नम,

ऐसे में कोई थामे अचानक ये दामन

जैसे बेवक्त बरसात बरसी हो आंगन।

कोई रंग नहीं बरसात का

फिर भी रंगीन हो जाती है ये फिज़ा,

सूखे, मुरझाए पत्तों पर जब गिरे सावन की बूंदे,

तब खिल के महक जाती है ये खिज़ा।

यूँ बादल का गर्जना और बिजली का कड़कना,

बारिश की बूंदों का मिट्टी पे गिरना

और मिट्टी की सौंधी सौंधी खूशबू से हवा का महकना,

देख के ये तसव्वुर हो रहा शुरू धड़कनों का हौले हौले मचलना।

तपती करारी धूप में झुक जायें जब बोझिल ये कंधे,

ना उमंग रहे, ना कोई सपने सजे,

जीवन लगे निराधार और हम हो जैसे कैद में बंधे,

टपके जब वर्षा की हल्की सी बूंदे,

बावरा ये मन सपनों के रंग भरे आंखें ये मूँदे।

मन लुभावन इस बरसते मौसम में,

इक कसक उठे मेरे सीने में,

पन्ने पलटू मैं जब अपनी यादों के,

बेचैनी भरे वो मेरे तन मन में,

आरज़ू है बस अब इतनी,

साथ ना छूटे तेरा अब इस जीवन में।

रमा शर्मा
मेरा पहला प्यार

जब भी सोचती हूँ, पहले प्यार के बारे में

एक सूरत मस्तिष्क पटल पर घूम जाती है

सोचती हूँ, कौन है ये जो हर सांस में मुझमें बस जाती है

पहले जी रही थी निर्जीव की तरह

सताती थी अस्तित्व पाने की विरह

उससे ही सूखे रेगिस्तान में बहार आती है

कौन है वो जिसकी खुशबू मुझमें महक जाती है?

उसके भीतर नौ महीने रही, उसने कुछ न कहा

हर दर्द वो मेरे लिए सहती रही

मैंने लिया उससे खान, पान और ज्ञान

पैदा हुई तो सबने कहा, ओहो ये तो लड़की है

किन्तु उसने मुझे दिलाया मान-सम्मान

कौन है जिसकी बातें अब तक मेरे

होठों पर आती है?

उसने मुझे सजाया संवारा

चोटी बनाकर, काजल लगाया

मैंने तो उसे बहुत सताया

किन्तु उसने हमेशा मुझे गले लगाया

कठिनाइयों में भी सच्चाई का रास्ता दिखाया

कौन है वो जिसकी बातें चूड़ियों सी

खनक जाती है ?

चली जाएगी जिस दिन वो मुझे छोड़कर

तन्हाइयों के मोड़ पर

तब ज़िन्दगी में नींद होगी, चैन होगा

पर करार ना होगा

सब कुछ होगा मेरे पास

पर मेरा पहला प्यार ना होगा

क्योंकि वही है मेरा पहला प्यार

मेरी माँ।

नए भारत की बात निराली है

विभिन्न धर्म, जाती और रंग हैं इसमें सिमटे हुए

पर हर लहू में देशभक्ति की लाली है

कितने वीर सपूत मर मिटे इसकी शान पर

हिन्दू - मुस्लिम मिलकर करते इसकी रखवाली है

मेरे देश की हर बात निराली है।

यूँ हुए मतभेद कईं, इसकी गोद में भी

पर वक्त पर सबने एक दूसरे की बाँहों में बाहें डाली है

कभी ईद पर भीनी-भीनी सेवियों की खुशबू

कभी दीपकों से जगमगाती दिवाली है

मेरे देश की हर बात निराली है।

आदतें बदली नहीं उन्होंने, घुसपैठ करने की

हमारे भी खून ने, ली खूब उबाली है

वैसे तो आदर-सत्कार के लिए जाने जाते हैं हम

पर दुश्मन के चेहरे से आँखें भी हमने नोंच डाली है

मेरे देश की हर बात निराली है।

माना की पिछले दो वर्ष नहीं कुछ ठीक रहे

ऐसे में हमारे मेडिकल स्टाफ ने कमान संभाली है

सामाजिक दूरी, टिके और मास्क के इस्तेमाल से

कोरोना ने भी हमसे मुँह की खाली है

मेरे देश की हर बात निराली है।

डर कर चुप बैठना हमने सीखा नहीं

घर में घुसकर हमने बदले की आग बुझाली है

किसकी मजाल जो हम पर नज़र गड़ाये

सर पर कफ़न बांधकर हमने सेना सजाली है

मेरे देश की हर बात निराली है।

एकता और अखंडता भरी हुई है इस मिट्टी में

स्त्री -पुरुष दोनों ने मिलकर देश की बागडोर संभाली है

हो विज्ञान, खेल, मनोरंजन या सौंदर्य प्रतियोगिता

हर क्षेत्र मैं भारतीयों ने बाज़ी मार डाली है

मेरे देश की हर बात निराली है।

गर्व है हमें इस नए भारत का वासी होने पर

इस देश की मिट्टी हमने माथे से लगा ली है

मरना नहीं, कुछ कर जाना है देश की खातिर

यही बात हमने धड़कन में बसाली है

मेरे देश की हर बात निराली है।

मेरे देश की हर बात निराली है।

रंजीता सहाय अशेष
मुझमे भी कहीं एक शहर बसता है

ज़िन्दगी भागती, दौड़ती, संभलती है

आँखे सूखे पत्ते सी रोती बिलखती है

रोम-रोम मेरा ऊँची इमारतों सा हँसता है

शायद मुझमे भी कहीं एक शहर बसता है।

काली लटें गुमान करने को मचलती है,

पर काया हर पल डरी, सहमी सिसकती है ,

मेरे भीतर भी अंतर्द्वंद धीरे-धीरे पनपता है,

शायद मुझमे भी कहीं एक शहर बसता है।

एक मन चकाचौंध की तरफ बढ़ता है,

तो दूजा संस्कारों में बरबस बंधता है,

क्लेश, कलह, काले धुएँ सा चारों तरफ पसरता है,

शायद मुझमे भी कहीं एक शहर बसता है।

आओ मिलकर 'नए भारत' का निर्माण करें

जहाँ जाति धर्म से ऊंचा मानवता का सिंहासन हो,

झूठ फरेब से हट कर मर्यादा का पालन हो,

वीर शहीदों की कुर्बानी का हर युवक गुणगान करे,

आओ मिल कर 'नये भारत' का हम निर्माण करें।

जहाँ पानी संचित करने के नित नए प्रयास करें,

दिव्यांगों की सब कद्र करें, ना कोई उनका उपहास करे,

गली मोहल्ले चौक चौबारे सब स्वच्छ रखने का आह्वान करें

आओ मिल कर 'नये भारत' का हम निर्माण करें।

जहाँ बंधुआ मजदूरी की भेंट कोई बचपन ना चढ़ पाये,

शिक्षा पर अधिकार सभी का, ये बात जन जन को समझाए,

जहाँ नारी के हर रूप का आदर सम्मान करें,

आओ मिल कर 'नये भारत' का हम निर्माण करें।

जहाँ फसल लहलहाती हो, और हर किसान खुशहाल रहे,

हरा भरा हर गांव शहर हो, प्रदूषण का न निशान रहे,

जहाँ नयी तकनीक के साथ, पुरानी संस्कृति पर अभिमान करें,

आओ मिल कर 'नये भारत' का हम निर्माण करें।

सलिल जैन

मरकज़-ए-सफ़्हात

मैं किताब-ए-मरकज़-ए-सफ़्हात हूँ,

कभी नाँव, कभी ख़त, कभी शायर का कलाम हूँ।

जुस्तजू-ए-ज़माना मगर चाक-ए-सफ़्हात हूँ,

कभी फ़ेहरिस्त, कभी ख़्वाहिश, कभी आशिक़ का पैग़ाम हूँ।

क्यों कुछ लोग सिर्फ़ ख़्वाब होते हैं .....

क्यों कुछ लोग सिर्फ़ ख़्वाब होते हैं
साथ हों तो हम लाजवाब होते हैं।
बिछड़े तो हम नाकामयाब होते हैं
क्यों कुछ लोग सिर्फ़ ख़्वाब होते हैं।।

वो हमरी सोच के बड़े निकट होते हैं
पर वास्तव में बड़े ही विकट होते हैं।
जब चाहो तब नहीं वो निकट होते हैं
जब ना चाहो तब तुरंत प्रकट होते हैं।।

घंटो, तो कभी क्षणभर के यार होते हैं
आसमाँ, तो कभी वो खाकसार होते हैं।
बेरंग, तो कभी रंगो की बहार होते हैं
कमजर्फ़, तो कभी आँखें चार होते हैं।।

दिखते पास, पर साये निहायत दूर होते हैं
खाली हाथ, पर हाथ बढ़ाने को मजबूर होते हैं।
दिमागी ख़लल, पर दिल से हमें मंज़ूर होते हैं
बेवफ़ा सही, पर कमबख़्त हमारा ग़ुरूर होते हैं।।
क्यों कुछ लोग सिर्फ़ ख़्वाब होते हैं
मदमस्त, मस्तमौला, बेमिसाल होते हैं।
सिर्फ़ ख़्वाब ही सही पर कमाल होते हैं
क्यों कुछ लोग सिर्फ़ ख़्वाब होते हैं।।

किताब

वो मुझे मिली किताबखाने में, जैसे कोई नयी किताब।

देखा उसको परखा उसको, जैसे कोई नयी किताब।

चटक रंग और कड़क काठी थी, जैसे कोई नयी किताब

सिर्फ़ जिल्द देख ना समझ आयी, जैसे कोई नयी किताब।

एतिहासिक तो कतई नहीं थी, ये किताब।

हाल फ़िलहाल, की रंगत लिए थी, ये किताब।

ज़ख़ीरा -ए - अल्फ़ाज़ लग रही थी, ये किताब।

कुछ और नहीं अफ़साना-निगार थी, ये किताब।

परिचय को हाथ बढ़ाया, जैसे हाथ में ली नयी किताब।

उसने अपना नाम बतलाया, लिए हाथ में एक किताब

सिर्फ़ पहला पन्ना पलटा था, अभी बची थी पूरी किताब।

फ़ेहरिस्त इतनी जज़्ब, ना छोड़ी गयी फिर वो किताब।

अभी पढ़ ही रहा था सुख़न पन्नो से भरी, वह हसीन किताब।

आयी आवाज़ किसी मरदूद की, वापस रखो सभी किताब।

सहम गया दिल सोच कर, कोई और ना ले जाए ये किताब।

बिछड़ने के ख़ौफ़ से, मैं चुरा लाया वह दिलकश किताब।

श्याम सुन्दर शर्मा
बीस साल पहले

आज इसी दिन, बीस साल पहले

आज इसी दिन, बीस साल पहले

मुझे शौर्य चक्र का तमगा मिला था

वीरगाथाओ के इतिहास मे

मेरा नाम हमेशा के लिया जुड़ा था

आज, कही किसी बक्से मे

जंग खा रहा होगा

वो खून से सिला शौर्य चक्र

जिसे मैंने सालो तक

शान से अपने सीने पर जड़ा था

पलटन के प्रेरणा कक्ष मे

टंगी मेरी तस्वीर

पर मिट्टी जमी होगी

कभी कोई पलट कर कभी देखता होगा

फिर साफ़ हो कर अगली धुल का इंतिज़ार

करती होगी मेरी तस्वीर

शौर्य चक्र मेरे नाम के साथ

मरणोपरांत भी जुड़ा रहेगा

शूरता की कमी तो

तमगे से पहले भी नहीं थी

आज, फिर क्यों बस एक थकान है

ना ही आँखों मे वो तूफ़ान है

इस वीराने मे मेरा दुश्मन कहा है

उससे कहो

अब और मेरे अंदर ना छुप

घात लगाना और घात तोडना

मुझे बैखूबी आता है

क्यों मेरा दुश्मन

बाहर निकल नहीं आता है

अंदर ही अंदर दीमक की तरह

मेरे वजूद को खोखला किये जाता है।

सुखदीप सांगवान
आम आदमी पिसता जाएगा

कहीं हैं क्या दिल में छुपी कुछ देशभक्ति,
कभी आहत होती हैं क्या अन्त:कर्ण की शक्ति,

कुछ देश प्रेम के अंश बचे हैं क्या ज़हन में,
या फिर विवेक बर्फ हो चला है आपके अन्तर्मन में,

क्या हुआ है आभास कभी एक अद्भुत सी घुटन का,
क्या महसूस की है नफरतों की आंधियों में वो चुभन,

क्या अन्तरात्मा कसमसाती है कभी,
जब 'टी वी' पर पकाई जाती हैं द्वेष और घृणा की 'कढ़ी',

क्या विक्षत होगा कभी अन्त:करण हमारा,
क्या विवेचित करेंगे हम कभी, चैतन्य हमारा,

कब तक बंदी रहेंगे हम टीवी की 'नफरती शामों' के,
कब झकझोरेंगे ईमान, इन चन्द 'विषमयी' एंकर-एंकराओं का,

हे जनमानस, उठो-जागो और हिम्मत कर अपनी निद्रा त्यागो,

झूठ, नफरत, वैमनस्य और ज़हर फैलाने वालों से उत्तर तो मांगो,

धज्जियां उड़ा दो इन नफरती सौदागरों के दुस्साहस की,
झलक तो दिखला दो इन्हें हिन्दुस्तानी शौर्य और साहस की,

अन्यथा देश में केवल द्वेष ही रह जाएगा,
चुनिंदा चापलूस ऐश करेंगे और आम आदमी, बस पिसता जाएगा।

सुशील दत्त 'देव'
ग़ज़ल - 1

ख़ाक ज़माना है सहरा, उसके आगे
उसकी आंखों का है पहरा, उसके आगे

वो कहे आग तो आग है दिल,
वरना क्या नहीं है दरिया, उसके आगे

है कोई ग़म के छोड़ बैठा हूँ
रफाकत-ओ-इबादत-ए-ख़ुदा, उसके आगे

शहर-ए-मक़तल के बाद है शहर-ए-इश्क़
हम जाएँ फिर भी पा-ब-जौलां , उसके आगे

ग़म-ए-जाना से परे भी हैं अहद इश्क़ के,
मिलती है ख़ाक में दुनिया, उसके आगे

खेल है उस बेदाद को दिल का दुखाना,
ज़ालिम भी लगता है मसीहा, उसके आगे

रिन्द उसकी नज़रों से ज़िन्दा हैं 'देव'
खाली लगता है मयखाना, उसके आगे

ग़ज़ल - 2

साक़ी तेरे बज़्म में किस्से वफ़ा ना हुई,
एक कली बिगड़ गयी, जो कभी खफ़ा ना हुई

एक ही काम सहल था, एक ही काम बना नहीं,
एक ही बात कहनी थी, वो बात बजा ना हुई

उसकी ज़ुबाँ पर आई जो, शीरीं वहीं ठहर गई,
ऐसी कोई घटा नहीं, जो उसपर फिदा ना हुई

है बढ़ा मायूस कितना, उसके शहर का चारागर,
उसके नज़र के मारों की, कोई दवा ना हुई

है ग़रीबी हिज्र की, दिल पर हाथ रख लिया,
तेरे बगैर कट गई, क्या वो सज़ा ना हुई

फिर है ज़ख़्म भर रहा, फिर हैं नाख़ून बढ़ रहे,
लानत आशिक़ों पर है, जो चाक कबा ना हुई

अहद-ए-शिकवा-ए-इश्क़ में, मैंने भी सर झुका लिया,
फिर 'देव' याद आ गया, फिर दुआ ना हुई

वर्षा रानी

आज की नारी आज की नारी हूं

तन्हा हूं, मगर अकेली नहीं हूं
उलझन में हूं, उलझी हुई नही हूं।

मन से सुंदर हूं, खुबसूरत नही हूं,
मुहब्बत बेपनाह है, इश्क में नहीं हूं।

दुखी हूं मगर, गम में डूबी हुई नही हूं ,
रास्ते में ठोकर खाई हूं, चलना भूली नहीं हूं।

मुस्कुरा कर, नज़र - अंदाज़ की हूं,
नज़रों से फिर भी, किसी को गिराई नहीं हूं।

आँखों में सपने सजाई हूं, किसी के ख्वाब तोड़ी नहीं हूं,
गिर कर कई दफा संभली हूं, किसी को गिराई नहीं हूं।

खिलाना जानती हूं, किसी के पैसे खाई नहीं हूं,
चलने की आदि हूं, किसी दौड़ में शामिल नहीं हूं।

सबकी नजर में हूं, किसी से नजर चुराई नहीं हूं,

शांति में हूं, शोर से घबराई हुई नहीं हूं।

प्रकृति की प्रेमी हूं, इंसानियत भूली नहीं हूं,
हां, कुछ अलग हूं मैं, पहले जैसे नहीं हूं।

कला है ये भी, जिंदगी जीने कि,
कुछ तजुर्बे बुन रही हूं, जीवन से हारी नहीं हूं,
लिखना पसंद है, लेकिन पढ़ने से हिचकिचाई नहीं हूं।

वन्दना यादव
फौजी की बेटी

कहाँ से हूँ मैं?

वे पूछते हैं "कहाँ से हूँ मैं?"

मेरा गांव, शहर, जिला या राज्य जिस पर

पूछते हैं सवाल बार-बार

कि कहाँ से हूँ मैं!

मम्मा का ग्रह प्रवेश हुआ था शादी के बाद

उत्तर प्रदेश में!

उन दिनों पोस्टिंग थी पापा की वहाँ।

मेरा जन्म गुजरात का

और

छोटी की पैदाइश बंगाल की।

दादी माँ ने साथ छोड़ा कश्मीर में

उससे पहले बाबा परलोक सिधारे

जब हमारी रिहाइश थी राजस्थान में!

हमने उम्र के अलग-अलग मोड़ पर

वे सभी घर, अस्पताल देखे दोबारा,

जहाँ याद रखे जाने वाले पायदान पर

रखा था कदम मेरे परिवार ने।

हम दोनों बहनों के

दसवीं-बारवीं के रिपोर्ट-कार्ड ही अलग-अलग जगहों के नहीं हैं,

आधार कार्ड में सिर्फ शहर अलग नहीं हैं,

राज्य और स्थानीय भाषाएं भी

हर पहचान-पत्र में अलग हैं।

अगर कोई चीज़ एक है तो वह हमारा भारतीय होना है

जो सारी तरह के कार्ड में

सबका, एक जैसा है।

शुरू से अब तक बदला नहीं कोई कार्ड, हमारी पहचान का।

एक ही है पहचान प्रमाणपत्र मेरे परिवार का।

हमारी बोलचाल की भाषा

हिन्दी-अंग्रेजी के साथ

अलग-अलग बोलियों में रची-बसी है।

वे इसे हिन्दुस्तानी कहें या कुछ और

पर कैंटोनमेंट में

हम इसे "अपनी भाषा कहते हैं।"

इन शब्दों में पहचान बसती है हमारी।

बोलने भर से हम पहचान जाते हैं

एक-दूसरे को

कौन, कहाँ-कहाँ रहा है, अब तक

कहाँ स्कूलिंग हुई या कॉलेज में पढ़े।

हम जाती में नहीं बंटे,

ना बंटते हैं, धरती के टुकड़ों पर।

हम किसी एक जगह के हैं ही नहीं,

हम हिन्दुस्तानी हैं।

हमारी यादों का समंदर बिखरा पड़ा है

समूचे देश में।

पूना में एक घर लिया था पापा ने

रिटायर्मेंट के बाद रहने को।

उन्हीं दिनों एडब्लूएचओ की लिस्ट में

बैंगलोर में भी आशियाना निकल आया।

अब कैसे बताएं कि कहाँ के बाशिंदे हैं हम!

सिविलियन दोस्त पूछते हैं, कहाँ से हूँ मैं?

घर कहाँ है हमारा?

समझना मुश्किल है कि वे पूछते क्या हैं?

पुश्तैनी मकान, या घर हमारा?

जो सरहदों की सीमाओं से अलग है!

कैसे कहूँ कि हम किसी एक राज्य या बोली के नहीं, समूचे देश के हैं।

हम हिन्दुस्तान के हैं, हम हिन्दुस्तानी हैं।

जब वे पूछते हैं "कहाँ से हूँ मैं?"

सिर्फ एक जवाब है मेरा, कि खालिस भारतीय हैं हम।

विनोद कुमार पंत
तबादला / पोस्टिंग

आए फिर एक नई जगह

सब कुछ नया जैसे नई सुबह

साथी, काम, स्थान, सब बदला

क्योंकि हमारा हुआ तबादला।

हमें हर वर्ष, पर होता स्थान बदलना

मिलना नए लोगों से फिर बिछड़ना

हम समय नई ठोकरें खाकर संभालना

हर कुछ दिन पर नई जगह को सवारना।

कहते हम खुद को बंजारे

सहते बिछड़न के अंगारे

ना बन पाते किसी के दुलारे

ज्यादा समय होते ना हम प्यारे।

नए लोग नई जगह नया माहौल

बदलता रहता है हमारा रोल

सब कुछ के साथ बदलता है मोल

हुए कहीं इज्जत कहीं खुले पोल।

जाने से पहले होता बहुत काम

पहुंचने पर भी करने पड़ते कई इंतजाम

सब कुछ ले जाते पर कुछ छोड़ जाते नाम

याद रखेंगें सभी आपका व्यवहार व काम।

पाकर उन्नति मिलता उसको इनाम

अच्छाइयों से छोड़ जाते गुण तमाम

पर कुछ लोग होते भी हैं हराम

दुर्गुणों के कारण होते हैं बदनाम

पड़ता है अपना सब कुछ समेटना

चाहते हैं काम का सब बटोरना

नियति होती कुछ भी बस लपेटना

हो सके जितनी भी उसे कुरेदना।

कभी साथ परिवार कभी अकेले

हर जगह मिलते नये मेले

पहुंचने पर मिलते अलग झमेले

हर तबादले पर कष्ट नए झेले।

इन्ही तबादलों से हमारा जीवन चलता

इनसे कभी कुछ समझता वह बदलता

काफी व्यापार इस पर है चलता।

नए लोगों से संस्था का रूप सवरता

निखरती भारत की अनेकता में एकता

नए लोगों से रूप बदलती सभ्यता

पकड़ती नई गति वहां की व्यवस्था

नए लोगों से पनपती नई महानता।

तबादले से होता है जीवन में बदलाव

सीखेंगे हम कि ना रहे एक जगह से लगाव

बनाएं हर कुछ दिन बाद नया पड़ाव

अच्छे कार्यों से बढ़ाएंगे नहीं जगह का भाव।

पुरानी जगह के साथ भूले भूले बुराइयां

नई जगह लेकर जाए सभी अच्छाइयां

मिले उन्नति पाए बधाइयां

नए माहौल में पहले खुशियां।

यासीन मोहम्मद
बारिश

गर्मी से तर बितर, तबियत हो रही थी मुश्किल।

ज़ुबां सूख गई, हर जीव हो चुका तंगदिल॥

पत्तों से नमी कुछ गायब सी हो गई।

धरती से खुशी कुछ ओझल सी हो गई॥

सूरज की गर्मी ने सबको किया परेशान।

सहा सबने गर्म हवाओं का प्रकोप और हुए बेजान॥

आया एक बादल घना, सूरज को बोला कुछ कानों में।

सूरज ने लिया एक कदम पीछे, सबका ध्यान गया आसमानों में॥

लगा मिलेगी कुछ राहत, यही सब सोचने लगे।

खुशी के आलम में सब मुस्कुरा कर झूमने लगे॥

तभी हवा ने अपना रुख कुछ इस तरह मोड़ा।

जान में जो जान आ रही थी, उसमें पड़ गया रोड़ा॥

उम्मीदों पर पानी फैलता जा रहा था।

खुशियों पर गर्मी का खतरा फिर से मंडरा रहा था॥

आया हवा का एक झोंका, कुछ कहना था उसे शायद।
महसूस हुआ धरती को, अब मिलने वाली है कुछ राहत।।

पहली बूंद जब पड़ी धरती पर, मुस्कुरा पड़े सारे पेड़ पौधे।
उत्साह में झूम उठा माहौल, पंछी लगे उड़ने और बच्चे मैदान में भागे।।

धरती और बूंदों के संगम ने कर दिया सबको दीवाना।
महक गया संसार, जब सुगंध ने कर दिखाया अपना कारनामा।।

पक्षियों ने छोटी छोटी बूंदों से अपनी प्यास बुझाई।
पत्तों ने खुद पर जमी धूल की कर दी धुलाई।।

इंतज़ार का वक्त, तकलीफों का दौर हुआ अब खत्म।
कई अरसों बाद सब पर हुआ कुदरत का रहम।।

बारिश का मौसम ले आया अनेक खुशियां।
बच्चे बूढ़े हुए निहाल और रसोई में बनी सेवइयां।।

झीलों और नदियों में आई एक नई लहर।
मछलियां और मेंढक खुशी से उछल पड़े इधर उधर।।
ले लो इस बारिश का मज़ा जी भर कर सभी।
बस आज ही का दिन है, ऐसे जी लो अभी।।

Photograph by Lt Col Salil Jain

Authors' Bio

AARYA KUMARI

Aarya Kumari, student of Journalism and Mass communication at Chandigarh University. She's been writing since 2020, she likes to write articles on social evils and patriotic poems. She's learnt a lot in this journey of writing and is still learning. She's a public speaker and has represented her institute at different levels. She has also done commentary of Multi Activity Display (Autumn Term 2021) at Officer's Training Academy, Gaya. Aarya loves exploring new things in life.

ABHISHEKANAND TRIPATHI

Maj Abhishekanand Tripathi is a serving army officer. With the efforts of his parents, his childhood was spent amidst Hindi literature. By the virtue of studying in Saraswati Vidya Mandir, his penchant for Hindi literature became stronger. He was commissioned in the Indian Army after military training at the National Defence Academy from 2009-2012 and at the Indian Military Academy from 2012-2013. His first book "Udgaar" was published in the year 2019 by Bluerose Publications. He is now working on his next poetry collection. Email: vidhuananda@gmail.com

ABHISHEK KUMAR SINGH

Lt Col Abhishek Kumar Singh is an alumni of Indian Military Academy and was commissioned in 70 Armoured Regiment on 07 Jun 2008. The officer hails from Lucknow and is 40 yrs old. He has done his schooling from Colvin Taluqdar's College Lucknow and he is B.Tech in Computer Science & Technology.He is an ardent listener & learner and his hobbies include poetry, sketching , reading psychology & philosophy. He is also part of various literati groups.

ADITYA PAWAR

Lt Col (Dr.) Aditya Pawar is a Surgeon in the Indian Army, an alumnus of the Scindia School and the prestigious Armed Forces Medical College, Pune. He pursued his Master's in General Surgery from Kolkata. His plays have been staged at various college and university levels and came out as winners. His first novel, *From the Fort Walls: How it Began* is based on his own teenage experiences. He has the distinguished honour of editing *Memoirs of Covid Warrior in Olive Green,* the book for Armed Forces. His poems are based on patriotism, romance and social issues. His poems have featured in *The Force Is With Us*, an international anthology. His father, Dr. Devendra Pawar 'Dev' is a Hindi poet whose poetry book titled *Sandhiyan Lekar* was published and released by the then President, Dr. A.P.J. Abdul Kalam (1998).

ABHYUDAY PRAKASH

Maj Abhyuday Prakash is an alumnus of Rashtriya Indian Military College, Dehradun. He joined the National Defence Academy in 2012 and finally got commissioned to Corps of Army Air Defence from IMA in 2016. He is an avid reader and a keen writer. He has also written various poems and articles for school and Academy Magazine too. Presently, he is posted in Pune.

ADITYA DESHMUKH

Maj Aditya Deshmukh is a veteran and has served in the armed forces from 2011-21. He was fortunate enough to have served at LAC, LOC, IB as well as AGPL in short ten years of his service and was one of the youngest to have accomplished that in his Regiment. He was commissioned in 5th Bn The Mahar Regiment. He is a voracious reader and writes poetry on various aspects of human tendencies. He is settled in Pune and doing campus head at a prestigious institute there.

AKANKSHA MODANI

Akanksha Modani, born in Jaipur, Rajasthan in 1981, is professionally an Electronics engineer and a core poet at heart. She started penning down her thoughts at the age of 15. Luring to understand life's little aspects, the prevailing confusions of teen age and growing up amidst a hunger to learn the distinctiveness of Birth and Death her amicable journey has culminated a collection of soul absorbing words. She wishes to publish her work soon for the world to read and analyse.

AKHILESH YADAV

Akhilesh Yadav is an Indian politician and national president of Samajwadi Party who served as the 20th Chief Minister of Uttar Pradesh from 2012 to 2017; having taken the oath at 38 years of age, he is the youngest person to have held the office. He was schooled at Rashtriya Military School, Dholpur, Rajasthan.

ANITA PANDA

Anita Panda is author of *Genesis* (2021), sister of a defence personnel and a Mumbai based passionate author-poet. Her work appears in anthologies like *Indian Poets*

United, We The World Poets, Living On, Amity Peace Poems, Times of India, Mumbai Mirror, DNA, New Woman, Atelier & eShe. She is a feisty crusader, determined to break through social stigmas that slot and judge a woman and striving to empower her in the still deeply patriarchal India. She is launching her debut book soon *Songs of My Soul*, a collection of 47 poems suffused with passion, emotion, courage and resilience of the human spirit. She is also a practicing Bodhisattva having encountered this powerful philosophy during a dark phase in her life that led to her spiritual awakening and her tryst with Buddhahood.

AVINASH SN

Lt Cdr SN Avinash is an alumnus of the 126th course, National Defence Academy. A proud Ex-Juliet, is serving in the Submarine Arm of the Indian Navy. The author is an avid reader and is fondly remembered by his course mates for his shenanigans during his time in NDA.

ANEETA SHARMA

Aneeta Sharma is an educator with 26 years of teaching experience in schools across the country. In 2021, she published a novel, *Home Run* and a poetry book, *A Handful of Dewdrops*. Her works have been published by Kitaab International, Indian Periodicals and Visual Verse on their platforms and her blogs appear under Random Musings @ TOI. Aneeta hails from a family which is steeped in military tradition and has her roots in Himachal Pradesh. She is a member of the Council for Global Education, Women's Indian Chamber of Commerce and Industry (WICCI).

ANKITA SRIVASTAVA

Lt Col Ankita Srivastava (retd) is born with a flair of natural narration. Having joined Army as an officer in 1993, she occasionally switched between her guns and pens. She hung her boots after 14 years of military life and walked beauty pageant ramps. She won Tanishq Big Memsaab 2008 and in Gladrags Mrs. India 2009 won the "Most Vivacious" sub award. She has contributed in 15 anthologies; authored 4 e-fictions on amazon kindle. Awards won are – *Tejaswini, SBI Excellence, Best Author, Veer Viraangna, Best Security Officer*. Her paperbacks are *Pink Scarecrow* and *Ahsas*. Her latest book is **From Olive Green to a Beauty Queen** published by Shrishti Publishers.

ASHWINI R SANE

Ashwini R Sane is a 'professional' Mom and an author of science fiction fantasy mythology Books. Her published works are: *The Adventures of Little Kanya* -The Sonic Reverberator (Shortlisted for AutHER awards 2023), Nakshatra of Ethos and the *Abodes of the Gods, The Terrorist Inquest*- a drama. The Poem 'The Search for Honesty' selected in AWWA (Army Wives Welfare Association Magazine/ Journal) Journal 2021. Winner of Times Animation Contest 2007-2008 conducted by Times of India. She loves to paint, listen to music and read books. She loves animals, nature and playing tennis.

ARTI CHOPRA

Arti Chopra was born in J&K and studied in St Mary's Presentation Convent. She did her graduation in Home Science from Delhi and got married to a fighter pilot in IAF. She completed her B.Ed. Degree while her two children were still small, keeping the uncertainty of her husband's profession in mind. In 2015, she published a book called *'My Life With The Boys In Blue'* which was written to create awareness of what being a service officer's wife entails. The sale proceeds of the book were donated towards the welfare of Air Force widows and their families via the Air Force Association. She worked for 3 years in an NGO doing fundraising for the underprivileged. Writing poetry, blogs, painting, cooking and watching cinema are her hobbies and occupies her pleasurably.

BALACHANDRAN NAIR

Balachandran Nair, a bilingual poet, translator, philanthropist, and social activist has served for 30 in CRPF. He has published four poetry anthologies in English and one in Malayalam language. He is published worldwide in 73 anthologies and has translated a Malayalam poetry anthology to English. His poems have been translated to 67 world languages. He has published a single -poem-fifty-languages poetry anthology titled 'Steal". In receipt of awards including Sahitya Academy Awards from Indian States Telangana and Gujarat. Captained a unique literary venture Haven Rendezvous in which more than 400 students from Govt. Schools were introduced to world arena of literature every day, continuously for 365 days of 2022 thereby creating a world record.

CHARU KALRA

Charu Kalra is a wife of an army officer and a postgraduate from Delhi University. She has been a former senior-level school instructor and content developer for an E-learning portal. She writes socially compelling women-oriented stories & poetry. Her work can be found in Momspresso, Readers' blog of the Times of India and articles in the Times Neighborhood of Patiala. Issues about caste, gender, religion, and ethnicity have always incited her to use the power of the pen and curate relevant and impactful ideas.

DEEPTI MENON

Deepti Menon is a wife of defence personnel. She has published 4 books, titled 'Arms and the Woman (Rupa Publishers), *Deeparadhana of Poems*, *The Shadow Trilogy - Shadow in the Mirror*, *Where Shadows Follow* and *Shadows Never Lie*, and *Classic Tales from The Panchatantra*. As a freelance journalist in Chennai, she was lucky enough to interview celebrities like Jeffrey Archer, Ruskin Bond and many. Deepti has always enjoyed writing thriller stories and has been published in around 20 anthologies, including *Unkahi: The Unsung* (Part 1) along with other noteworthy writers. Her latest book 'Defying Destiny: Nalini Chandran – A Life Sketch' (Logos Books) is a life sketch on Ms. Nalini Chandran, her mother who is a renowned educationist.

DILIP MOHAPATRA

Commodore Dilip Mohapatra, VSM, a Navy Veteran from Pune is a well acclaimed poet and author in contemporary English. His poems and stories regularly appear in many literary journals and anthologies worldwide. He has six poetry collections, one short stories collection and two non-fictions to his credit. He is the recipient of the International Naji Naaman Literary Awards, 2020 and has been granted the honorary title of 'Member of Maison Naaman pour la Culture'. He holds two Master's degrees, in Physics and in Management Studies. His website may be accessed at dilipmohapatra.com.

DV SANTOSH MEHER

Lt Col Santosh Meher is a person of poetic inclination who gets inspired by a myriad of subjects, including love, motivation, comedy, nature- anything that tickles, stimulates, excites or stirs the thoughts of his mental recesses. Till a while ago, he savoured his works as a personal passion. It is only recently that he broke free from the shackles of his hesitation and decided to make public his musings of poetry and becoming a part of this beautiful World of Words. His passion to travel enhances his horizon of imagination, thus adding varied colours and flavours to the poetic canvas. He attempts to write in English as well as Hindi

GAUTAM NANDREKAR

Gautam Nandrekar, fondly known as Ashblog on Instagram, since that is his Instagram handle name. A software engineer, gave up my 9 years of corporate career to start my own Food business in Goa. An avid Military/ Defence photographer, he travels across India to capture the amazing Aircrafts the Indian Air Force has, and various other Army and Navy related events. It's his passion to convey or to tell a story about Indian Defence Forces through his lens and has been doing it for many years now. Writing poems comes naturally to him and very spontaneously. He takes immense pride in being a Patriotic Indian and continue to portray the defence forces in their true sense till his heart beats.

GD BAKSHI

Major General (Dr.) G.D. Bakshi (retd) is a combat veteran of many skirmishes on the LOC and counter-terrorist operations in Jammu & Kashmir and Punjab. He has held many prestigious posts in several military and non-military organizations. He is a motivational speaker and has authored 37 books on war, military power, poetry and riddles of the Vedas. His poetry books include *Freedom is an Eagle: Poems from an Outpost* that celebrates philosophical musings of lonely soldiers coping with extreme peril and danger on the high Himalayas, far from their loved ones and *Dances with the Cranes* celebrates the magic and mystery of death and rebirth. He has two children and lives in Gurgaon with his wife Suneeta.

GAURAV BHATIA

Col Gaurav Bhatia, Ph.D., a veteran Scholar Warrior, delves passionately into Disaster Management and Risk Reduction. His published works, include *Biological Disasters – The City Beautiful Un(Prepared)*, research papers and fiction writings which grace prestigious peer reviewed international/ national journals and multiple anthologies. Post superannuation, he dedicates his expertise to Public Health and has been the State Lead (Immunization) at Clinton Health Access Initiative (CHAI), William J Clinton Foundation and is now Senior Advisor with the Empower School of Health, Geneva. He is based out of Lucknow, Uttar Pradesh.

GOPAL PURDHANI

Gopal Purdhani was immersed in the world of learned literature since his childhood and started participating in the monthly program of his poems from Jalandhar Radio Station. In his youth, the well-known litterateurs of that time, such as Mr. Shiv Batalvi, Mr. Ajit Singh Dag and He learned a lot by coming in contact with Mrs. Amrita Pritam ji etc. He was a military officer for 30 years and after his retirement, he was made a 'Special Metropolitan Magistrate' from the recognized Delhi High Court, where he remained for 7 years and retired at the age of 65. After that, he was the chairman of a higher education institution. He has published 14 books.

HARISH CHANDRA JOSHI

Capt Harish Chandra Joshi commissioned into Engineer Regiment. He belongs to Distt Almora state Uttarakhand presently posted at Prayagraj.Poetry writing is his Hobby.He has received an award for poetry writing competition which was organised by the NDA on the occasion of completing its glorious 75 Years.

HARNOOR GREWAL

Harnoor Grewal is a teenaged published writer, poet and passionate photographer running on an overwhelming urge to capture the essence of moments and add meaning to it by her words. She is a volunteer at various NGOs, through which she wishes to achieve the goal of making India an educated & empowered country. She also wishes to bring positive changes through her writing by uniting articles ranging from the political world to the density of law reforms and its effects on the common man.

INDU TOMAR

Indu Tomar is a lawyer, poetess, life coach, social worker, an entrepreneur and wife of an army officer. She was an NSS trainee and participant for five years. Partnered with the state of Rajasthan for singularity and was honored with the award of 'Lohaghar Gaurav'. She has been contributing towards the welfare of the families of the soldiers as a member of AWWA since 2007. She has been a part of various NGOs and the Principal of Army Special Children's School 'ASHA'. In 2018, she was invited by the Dept of Arts and Culture South Africa Durban Province to inspire artisans and other women's groups. Presently, she is contributing to the society through awareness campaigns and other forms and gives motivational talks online and offline. She has recently published her poetry collection, "Kavya Srijan".

ITIKA KAHLON VIRK

Daughter from a family of educationists, wedded to the olive greens, Itika has had an array of experiences amply wide so as to encompass the vividness of the Nature and the uniqueness of the human species. Schooling from a Convent school, Itika secured her Bachelor's degree with Hons. in Home Science and a Bachelor's in Education from Punjab Agriculture University & her Masters in English from Punjab University. The poems in her collection are autobiographical besides being based on Nature. Here, Itika contributes a poem very special and dear to her - "My Heart n My Soul". It's a poem Itika wrote for her daughter on the tenth birthday.

INDU VASISHTHA

Mrs. Indu Vasishtha, 72, is the principal of a prestigious school and likes to write, read and to sing. Her qualifications include B.A. (hons) economics, M.A. economics, M. com. and B.ed. She is passionate about writing and had started early on in life. She is a nature loving person. Mrs Indu taught in a school for 20 years before being promoted to the position of the principal. Having emerged from all the hardships and battles of life as a victor, she writes poems and essays portraying her experiences in the form of words.

JITENDRA SINGH

Lt Col Jitendra Singh, an alumnus of the IMA was commissioned in Corps of Engineers in Dec 2001. He is Post Graduate in Geotechnical Engineering from IIT Madras and MBA(HR) from Amity University. As a young Lieutenant, officer took part in Op Parakram and thereafter deployed for UN Msn in Ethiopia-Eritrea. The officer has thorough experience in mega construction activities specialising in airfield runways and Hangar construction. He was posted as instructor, SEMT Wing in the prestigious College of Military Engineering, Pune. The literary bug caught the officer early and has been writing for various newspapers and magazines. His renowned works include 'Sarhad Aur parinda', 'Shinjar dekhna hoga', 'Mein Bindu huun', 'The hero detailed'.

JHANVI ATRI

Jhanvi Atri is a charismatic 11th grader daughter of an army officer looking to leverage her inclination towards computer science in a professional environment. She has a passion for public speaking and writing poetry and has written on diverse topics from personal experience to fictional genres. MUNing and debating have also been a part of her high school journey. Besides being a published author, Jhanvi reads books- fiction and non-fiction. She has interned at an organisation pertaining to different social issues. Poetry is her way of letting things off her mind and uses imagery to describe them in free verse form.

J K BHAGWAT

Dr. JK Bhagwat served as Associate Professor of English at the National Defence Academy, Pune from 1979 to 2006. He worked as editor of NDA Journal and the Chief Commentator of the passing out parade of the academy. He was a Cadet Counsellor of November squadron and later fourth battalion. He is settled now settled in Pune. He can be reached at jkbhagwat@hotmail.com

JYOTIRMOY GHOSAL

Col Jyotirmoy Ghosal is an alumnus of the National Defence Academy and commissioned in 4 JAT and Commanded 5 JAT & 114 TA (JAT). He was also the Dy Commandant & CI of JAT RC (2007-2009). Post retirement, he was CEO & Secretary of the prestigious MB Club, Lucknow (2015 to 2017). His War Accounts are part of two Anthologies, *"How the Wind Blew"* and *"Valiant Were Their Deeds"* published by *Sabre & Quill Publishers*. His poems have been published by *"Poetry Planet Publishing House"* in their Winner Poems' Anthologies *"Born to Dream"*, *"Dancing with Death"*, *"Spotlight"* and *"Plaisir D' Amour"*. His anecdotal stories and poems are part of three other anthologies. His book "Till The Last Breath - *Soft Sentiments of a Steeled Soldier*" has been published by Impish Lass Publishing House.

KETAKI PIMPLEKHARE

Ketaki Pimpalkhare was born in Pune. She completed her Bachelor's in Fine Art from the Directorate of Art, Bombay's G.D. Art program and studied photography from Fergusson College, Pune. Pimpalkhare then moved to the UK where she studied Creative Writing from SouthShields. Later, she got a Master's in Fine Arts from Women's University, Pune and worked in the field of advertising & event management. Her has been showcased in art galleries worldwide from 1999. She is married to a restaurateur Shekhar Pimpalkhare and has a son.

KUMUD MISHRA

Kumud Mishra is an Indian actor in Hindi cinema. He is an alumnus of Rashtriya Military School Belgaum, Karnataka and has graduated from National School of Drama, Delhi. Mishra has played supporting roles in the films *Filmistaan, Revolver Rani, Jolly LLB 2, Raanjhanaa, Badlapur, Bangistan, Airlift, MS Dhoni: The Untold Story, Sultan, Tiger Zinda Hai, Rukh, Aiyaary, Mulk, De De Pyaar De, Article 15, Bharat, Thappad, Sooryavanshi* and *Tadap*.

KRISHNA KUMAR

Air Commodore BS Krishna Kumar, KC (retd), had his schooling in Sainik School Kazhakootam. He Joined National Defence Academy as an Air Force Cadet. After successful completion of flying training at AFA, was commissioned as a Helicopter Pilot. During a career spanning 34 Years, he held many important appointments including Command of Helicopter Units at Carnicobar and UN Mission Congo, Director Plans at Air HQ, PD Training at NDA, Air Officer Commanding of an Operational Base and PD Helicopter Operations, Air HQ. He was Conferred the KIRTI CHAKRA, by the President of India for conspicuous act of Gallantry in saving over 300 people during Tsunami at Carnicobar. He is an avid writer and motivational speaker.

LILY SWARN

Lily Swarn is a multilingual poet, author, columnist, gold medallist, university colour holder, radio show host and a Peace Ambassador. *A trellis of Ecstasy, Lilies of the Valley, The Gypsy Trail* and *History on My Plate* are her highly acclaimed books in different genres. She has over 50 international and national awards to her credit and her poetry has been translated into over 16 languages. She is wife of Colonel (Rtd) SS Swarn, 58 Regular, Regiment of Artillery currently settled in Chandigarh. He is 48 Course, NDA.

MAMTA PANDIT

Mamta Pandit is wife of an army officer and has a 9 yr old daughter. She is MSc (Comp Sci). After working as a software engineer for around 8 years, at present, she is performing her family and army related social responsibilities very well. She was awarded with AWWA excellence award in 2018 from South Western Command, Jaipur. With these responsibilities, she enjoys writing and reading. She is associated with as a co-editor with magazine *Mahi Sandesh*, published from Jaipur. She is a book/movie reviewer and writes about women issues. She has a keen interest in poetry-writing and her works have been published in magazines & websites.

MONISHA RASTOGI

Monisha Rastogi is spouse of a naval officer, a teacher by profession and a blogger by choice. A mother of two teenage boys, she is always on her toes. She has travelled the world and postings all over the shore have made her pragmatic and accommodating. Navy has chiselled her into a beautiful human being who respects others opinions and does not believe in imposing her wishes on others. She blogs on varied topics and readers have often compared her simple heart touching works to Sudha Murthy's style of writing. There is no better compliment than this. Her poems have been published recently in the book *Changed Forever*.

NAVDEEP MULTANI

Col Navdeep Multani, an army veteran, is an avid photographer and compulsive traveller. He considers photography his form of meditation. He loves documenting the rich legacy of monuments through his lens, such that their photographs tell stories. He also indulges in short stories and poetry writing. Having served the country for over three decades, he hung his boots in 2021 and is now settled in Panchkula, until the next adventure comes calling.

NANDITA DE NEE CHATTERJEE

Nandita De nee Chatterjee is a Defence daughter and grew up in various Air Force stations. She did her Master's from

Jadavpur University. She was a freelance journalist writing in The Telegraph and later joined Economic Times and continued writing for mainstream news dailies. Her work covered children, welfare, labour, climate, human rights, nature and human-interest subjects. She taught Media Ethics in MA Journalism Dept at the University of Calcutta. She is a Co-Author in 63 Anthologies including 6 Coffee Table Books. She is also the Editor of 5 literary books and 2 literary journals. She's received numerous literary awards and 2 Peace Ambassador Awards. She's a Senior Editor with Chrysanthemum Chronicles Publications.

NAVNEET GREWAL

Navneet Grewal is a published author, qualified language teacher and a freelance content creator. She has published stories and poems in thirteen international and national anthologies with leading publishing houses. Her first book 'Our Hearts We Pen 'is a poetry collection co- authored with her teenage daughter. A member of the Chandigarh Literary Society (CLS) she has compered in many poetry as well as literary events. Content marking for two online websites, voiceover for a yoga foundation, research paper submission for crowd management, editor for a women empowerment platform she has written for the Hindustan times as well.

NITYA SHUKLA

Nitya Shukla is wife of an army officer, MSc in biochemistry and has been writing since childhood. Professionally she started writing from 2017. She has been awarded as one of "51 IN FINANCIAL WOMEN OF RAJASTHAN 2020" for contribution to Hindi literature world. She is also a winner of national poetry competition organised by the poetry Society of India 2019 and Indira Gandhi International youth award by central Ministry of youth affair and sports. She has been an editor in Indian literary magazine for 2 years and has hosted a show on Hindi literature from an international radio station of Chicago. Presently, she is working as principal of Colaba Army pre–Primary School one STC Jabalpur.

PAROMITA MUKHERJEE OJHA

Dr. Paromita Ojha is a wife of an Air Force officer, a voracious reader, passionate painter/crafter, and philanthropist. She is a participating author/poet of more than thirty- five national /International short story and poetry anthologies. She is a Winner of multiple literary contests. Participated and presented more than 21 research papers on Literature/HR/ Cultural Studies. Her Book of poetry titled 'Sylvan Fragrance' available on all major online platforms. Regularly expresses her thoughts on paromitamukherjeeojha.wordpress.com

PRAGYA BAJPAI

Dr. Pragya Bajpai is a proud mother, poet, artist, and academic at the National Defence Academy, Pune. She is a post-graduate from Lucknow University and holds a Ph.D. in English Literature from Banaras Hindu University. Her debut book of poems is *A Potpourri of Proverbs* (2021) and her second poetry collection is titled *Conversation on Cue* (2023) co-authored with Shefali Nautiyal. She has co-edited three anthologies titled *Unkahi: The Unsung* (2021), *The Force is With Us* (2022) and *Memoirs of Covid Warriors in Olive Green* (2022) to celebrate the armed forces. She has also co-edited a collection of Hindi poems called *Dabe Paanv*

(2022). Her poems have appeared worldwide. Her poem, 'On the Death of Kindness' featured in the Outlook has got international recognition and has been translated into Hindi, Bengali, Russian and Persian.

PRAVIN RAGHUVANSHI (IN)

Captain Pravin Raghuvanshi NM is an ex-Naval Officer and alumnus of *IIM Ahmedabad*. He served as a Senior Advisor in prestigious Supercomputer organisation C-DAC, Pune. He has translated over 100 Bollywood songs for various International forums as a mission for the global viewers and has also translated works for Shri Narendra Modi, the Hon'ble Prime Minister of India, which was highly appreciated by him. He is a member of 'Bombay Film Writer Association'. He is also the English Editor for the e-Abhivyakti. As a prolific writer, poet and 'Shayar', he participates in literature fests and 'Mushayaras'. He presided over the "Session Focused on Language and Translation" and also presented a research paper in the conference was organized by *Delhi University* in collaboration with New York University and Columbia University.

PRAVESH DHAYAL (IN)

Lieutenant Commander Pravesh Dhayal is an alumnus of the 130th (Golf) course of the National Defence Academy, Pune. The naval officer is a submariner. He started writing Hindi poetry during his academy days and has passionately nurtured his writing. He enjoys Horse Riding and playing Golf among other sports. He believes that a soldier fights because he loves those standing behind and beside him.

PIYUSH SHARMA

Piyush Sharma is the brother of Colonel Ashutosh Sharma 'Sena Medal'. You live in Jaipur. In the early days of life, both you and your brother wanted to serve the country by becoming soldiers. Ultimately your brother Ashutosh Sharma joined the army and became immortal forever by sacrificing his life for the country. Like your brother, you are serving the country like a soldier by staying outside the uniform and will continue to cooperate in it.

POOJA ATRI

Pooja Atri is a diligent home maker and wife of an army officer who manages her time juggling between various self-growth tasks. She is an avid reader with high interests in spiritual books. As a result of her inclination towards meditation, she has also completed an Art of Living course. Her qualifications include MA (Eng) LLB. Ms Pooja has been to district courts for few years as well for scheduled practices. She sings and dances her way through life and has an outgoing nature. She also plays table tennis to keep up with her physical well-being. She goes on trips to new places around nature as such historical bases attract her the most. Her passion for Hindi poetry has given her an in-depth knowledge of the divine power as well as the various other topics she writes on.

PRIYA KHANNA

An offspring of two fauji doctors, Priya Khanna is now a full-time, stay-at-home fauji wife and mother to a teen terror and a gorgeous golden cocker spaniel. When she's not reading,

Priya Khanna is likely bingeing on a crime series on Netflix and reminiscing about the time when she was jetting all over the world for her work as an instructional designer with a Gurgaon MNC. She loves to write down her personal experience and relish over it from time to time.

RAMA SHARMA

Major Rama Sharma is serving in Military Nursing Services since 2012; currently posted at Jaipur. She identified her passion for writing poetry at the age of 10. She studied at Jawahar Navodaya Vidyalaya, Sawai Madhopur. Prior to joining the Army, she did Bachelor's in English, Philosophy and Economics. In 2008, she got selected in College of Nursing, Armed Forces Medical College. She has won various interschool and intercollege competitions for creative writing and poetry recitation. In 2011, she was nominated as the best speaker of AFMC. She won 1st position in On-the-Spot Poetry Writing and Recitation in National TNAI Biennial Conference representing Maharashtra State. She is married to a Naval officer and has a 3-year-old daughter. She intends to publish her collections in future.

RANJEETA SAHAY ASHESH

Poetpreneur Ranjeeta Sahay Ashesh is a proud Army wife, running PAN India Poetry Organization KSHITIJ, she is An Author of two Books, certified Life Coach, Mrs India Delhi NCR Mrs Most Talented 2018, International Poetess and have been honoured with many prestigious Awards.

RAJ KRUSHNA MISHRA

Group Captain RK Mishra (retd), served 40 years in Air Force mainly as a Para Jump/ Sky-diving Instructor training the Parachute Regiment. He has a passion for singing and poetry, composes in English, Hindi and Odia. He is known for translation and collaborative poems with number of poets. In 2018, he has published his anthology *Rhythmic Mind* containing 100 love poems.

REENA SINGH

Reena Singh has more than 37 years' experience in senior editorial positions in The Times of India (TOI) and Genpact. She was Deputy Editor with TOI's spiritual newspaper, The Speaking Tree, where she spent nine years.

RENUKA SHUKLA

Renuka Shukla born on 30 September in a small town in Arunachal Pradesh. She is an educationist by profession, graduated from Lucknow University, Awadh Girls Degree College and has been teaching & counselling privileged and unprivileged masses for the last 35 years. She has contributed to the society in various forms as well as through her writings on relevant issues. She lives in Lucknow with her husband who served as a medical officer in the Indian Army.

ROOPALI SIRCAR GAUR

Dr. Roopali Sircar Gaur wife of an army officer is a lifelong teacher, poet-performer, writer, environmentalist, and social justice activist, who comes from a family of four generations and over 100 years in military service. Roopali retired as Associate Professor of English from Delhi University. She is a widely published columnist and writer, featured worldwide. Her poems are also housed at Stanford University's Digital Humanities initiative, *Life in Quarantine: Witnessing Global Pandemic,* and in the University of Bath's *Transnational* project. She is the Consulting Editor for *Different Truths,* an online global participatory journal, and the Poetry Editor for the *Aspiring Writers' Society.* She holds a PhD. in English Literature from Jawaharlal Nehru University, New Delhi.

RUPA RAO

Rupa Rao fell in love with words and wordsmithing when her adored larger-than-life father, recited poetry in his sonorous voice. She recalls being mesmerized as a seven-year-old. She holds an MBA and Law degree from erstwhile Bombay; and has been part of the corporate world in India and USA. Her experience spanning industries, continents, and mentoring enriches her. She cherishes the privilege of traveling extensively as an army child, loves nature walks, and meaningful exchanges. She misses her cheerleader parents who supported her writing passion. Her precious twins, a boy and girl, and her sister are her soft place to fall along with her partner. She is published worldwide and moderates online writing group. She will be publishing her poetry collections in the near future.

SAHANA AHMED

Sahana Ahmed is wife of an army officer is a poet and a novelist based in Gurugram. She is the author of *Combat Skirts* (Juggernaut, 2018) and the editor of *Amity: Peace Poems* (Hawakal, 2022). Her work has been published in the journal of the International Flash Fiction Association (IFFA), Yearbook of Indian Poetry in English, and The New York Times, among others. For more information, please visit her website: www.sahanaahmed.com

SALIL JAIN

Lieutenant Colonel Salil Jain is a Hindi poet and a serving Indian Army Officer with 18 years of experience. He is an alumnus of Cadet Training Wing, Pune and Indian Military Academy, Dehradun. He was commissioned in 2003. The officer has published his poems in various online magazines and presented his poems in online poetry meets. He has a penchant for Urdu language. He spends quality time with his family and loves to socialise with his friends. He believes in deep connections and long-lasting relationships. He is soon going to publish his solo Hindi poetry collection. Insta handle: salil_sajal

SANJEEV SETHI

Sanjeev Sethi is son of a defence personnel and has authored seven books of poetry. His latest is Wrappings in Bespoke (The Hedgehog Poetry Press, UK, August 2022). He has been published in over thirty countries. His poems have found a home in more than 400 journals, anthologies, and online literary venues. He is the recipient of the Ethos Literary Award 2022. He is the joint winner of the Full Fat Collection Competition-Deux, organized by The Hedgehog Poetry Press, UK. He edited Dreich Planet #1, an anthology of Indian poets for Hybriddreich, Scotland, in December 2022. He lives in

Mumbai, India. Twitter @sanjeevpoems3

Insta handle: sanjeevsethipoems

SEEMA AHIRA

Seema Ahira is a daughter of an army personnel and an expat Indo Canadian; having spent her childhood and formative years in the beautiful twin cities of Hyderabad and Secunderbad. She writes poetry to express her thoughts and feelings; at times incorporating social issues or concerns. She enjoys reading, gardening and loves to cook for her family and friends. She loves to sing although how well she sings is up for debate. She has been published in major international anthologies.

SHYAM SUNDER SHARMA

Lieutenant Colonel Shyam Sunder Sharma is a decorated and War wounded veteran. He holds a Bachelor's of Art Honours and a Master's degree in English. He is an avid poet, keen birdwatcher and nature lover. He was a Guest Poet from India at Fermoy International Poetry Festival at Ireland in August 2013. He runs a vibrant poetry group, Poets, Artists Unplugged which has published 4 international anthologies. His poems have been published in numerous anthologies, magazines and e-zines in India and abroad. His first poetry compilation titled *Adrift* was released in 2019 and is available on Amazon.

SIDDHANT KAUSHAL

Siddhant Kaushal is a son of Army officer and a successful and popular Hindi film lyricist and singer Bollywood.

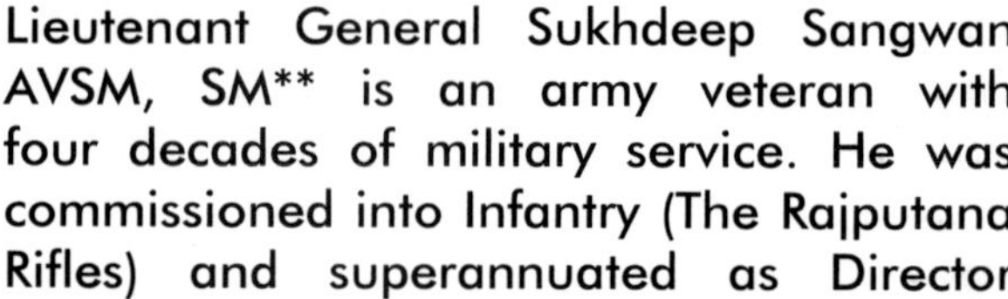

SUKHDEEP SANGWAN

Lieutenant General Sukhdeep Sangwan AVSM, SM** is an army veteran with four decades of military service. He was commissioned into Infantry (The Rajputana Rifles) and superannuated as Director General (DG) of the oldest Para Military Force, Assam Rifles. He has been a regular contributor to various professional magazines and was the Founder Editor of "SYNERGY", a magazine published by Centre of Joint Warfare and Studies (CENJOWS), New Delhi for which he was awarded the Chairman Chiefs of Staff Committee's Commendation Card in 2008. The General had authored a book titled *Integrated Force Projection by India* and was also associated with "Comprehensive National Power" published by CENJOWS. His poetry book titled *Random Thoughts* was launched in Jan 2021. The General has also written the lyrics of some of the promotional videos of the ASSAM RIFLES, the most popular being the "Tribute to Indian Army" (Ae Hind ki Sena naman tujhe).

SHYAMOLA KHANNA

Shyamola Khanna wife of (Late) Air commodore MD Khanna has been a teacher all her life, teaching English at all the various Indian Air Force schools where her husband's postings took them. She is a freelancing journalist /writer and continues to write for magazines as well as teach English and soft skills at engineering colleges and MBA schools. She is a published author of three books: *The COW in Kargyll* (2016), *The Lahore Connection* (2019), a collection of women centric short stories. And her latest *'From Mukherji to Malhotra'*. She continues to learn art and photography and remains an avid traveller.

SUNIL KAUSHAL

Sunil Kaushal is 78 years old daughter of a fourth-generation army officer poet, author, translator and editor awarded the Nassim award for her memoirs *"Gypsy Wanderings & Random Reflections"*, has been translated into French, Greek, German, Arabic and Chinese. She has been awarded with number of awards major once are the Nassim Award for nonfiction prose 2018 and the Enchanting News Award. She has featured in Limca Book of Records as part of Amravati poetic 2018 and has has also featured in the Golden Book of World Records. Presently she is busy compiling Part 2 of her memoirs *"Gypsy Wanderings & Random Reflections"*.

SUNIL DUTT 'DEV'

Lieutenant Sunil Dutt is an Indian Navy Officer who writes with the name pen name "Dev". He started writing poems at age of 14 and practiced Urdu poetry particularly ghazal. Mirza Ghalib, Mir Taqi Mir, Faiz Ahmad Faiz and Ahmad Faraz are some of his favourite poets and also the inspiration behind his poetry. He Believe in the classical ghazal and he endeavour to keep it alive and make it reach more and more art lovers.

SUJATA PARASHAR

Sujata Parashar is a Bestselling novelist, short-story writer and poet, became widely popular with her 'Pursuit' novel series and has so far written 12 books across genres. Her first poetry collection, *"Poetry Out and Loud"* (2012) won the *BtB Best Poetry Book* award. Later, she came out with its sequels, *POAL – II* (2013) and *POAL – III* (2014). Sujata was recognized as one of the

Women Achievers of 2021 by Apeksha Sandesh News. She has also been the recipient of the *100 Women Faces 2018* award and other literary awards including the PVLF Author Excellence Award 2022 that she received for her nonfiction, *Going Solo- Raising Happy Kids*, a hand guide on single parenting. www.sujataparashar.in

SWATI PAL

Swati Pal, wife of a defence personnel, Professor and Principal, Janki Devi Memorial College, University of Delhi. Author of several books on theatre, creative and academic writing, her newspaper articles articulate her views on education. Her poems appear in several anthologies, and has a collection entitled *In Absentia* and an edited volume called *Living on*. She is the Vice Chair of the Indian Association for Commonwealth Literature and Language Studies. She is the Delhi State Chair for the G100 Wing for World Peace of the Women Economic Forum. She has been the recipient of several awards such as a Lifetime Achievement Award for contribution in the area of educational administration by Women's Agency for generating Employment in 2017; Exceptional Women of Excellence in Academia, 2017 Award.

TULIKA NIYOGI

Tulika Niyogi married to Colonel Mihir Niyogi, a retired Indian Army doctor is a chemistry postgraduate with over 15 years' experience in education. Tulika has talent and passion for music, dance, art and choreography. She is an enthusiastic and dedicated educator who has vast experience of working with a variety of NGOs and educational institutions. Her poetry and articles are featured in several international fora. Presently is a coordinator and Delhi state facilitator for SPIC MACAY (Society for the Promotion of Indian Classical Music And Culture Amongst Youth), a voluntary youth movement.

TANUSHREE PODDAR

Born in New Delhi, wife of a defence officer, Tanushree worked in the corporate sector for 8 years before she quit the rat race to write. A well-known travel writer and novelist, she is passionate about traveling and writing. Tanushree has written many nonfiction books before moving to fiction and has published 17 novels. Among her books are *Nurjahan's Daughter, Boots Belts Berets, On the Double, Escape from Harem, Solo in Singapore, A Closetful of Skeletons, Before you Breathe, No Margin for Error, The Teenage Diary of Rani Laxmibai, The Girls in Green, An Invitation to Die, Spooky Stories, More spooky Stories,* and *Ambapali. Decoding the Feronia Files,* written by her, is the first Indian Cli Fi thriller. Three of her books, *Boots Belts Berets, A Closetful of Skeletons,* and *The Girls in Green,* are being adapted into web series. She lives in Pune.

TOOLIKA RANI

Squadron Leader Toolika Rani is an Ex-Indian Air Force Officer, Mountaineer (Everest Climber), International Motivational Speaker (TEDx), and academician. She is the G-20 Brand Ambassador of Uttar Pradesh (Higher Education), Election Commission's voter awareness program SVEEP in 2022 U.P. Assembly elections, and is the Ambassador of India, Women Empowerment Committee, in World Leader Summit. Her book *'Beyond That Wall: Redemption on Everest'* has received Sahitya Shree Award, and Young Writer Award from Military Literature Festival. She is the co-author of two books *Humans of Nurture Life* and *Reach for the Sky and the Stars*. Her co-authored book *Healing and Growth* (2022) was published from USA. She has been felicitated with 17 awards. tulich83@gmail.com

VARSHA RANI

Varsha Rani is the wife of an Indian Army officer and is interested in Hindi writing. She is a resident of Bihar whose heart resides in Marine Drive. You believe that threading words is easy but choosing words is difficult. You try to choose good words every day and put your thoughts down on paper every day. Through poetry, you connect yourself with nature, human spirit and your experiences.

VANDANA YADAV

Writer, motivational speaker, anchor and social worker Vandana Yadav was born Bikaner and currently lives in Delhi. Apart from the novel *'Shuddhi'* published recently from Bharatiya Jnanpeeth, the author's novel *Kitne Morcha* on the wives of the soldiers became very popular. *Ab Manzil Meri Hai*, apart from the Motivational book, many of your books have been published. Vandana continues to write essays on All India Radio and newspapers and magazines on mental health, women's rights and other contemporary topics

VANDANA PARASHAR

Vandana Parashar is a postgraduate in Microbiology, an educator and a haiku poet. Her haiku, senryu and tanka have been published in many national and international journals of repute and has won her many prizes and accolades. Her haiku was also shortlisted for the prestigious Touchstone Award 2020 She is an associate editor of haikuKATHA, one of the editors of Poetry Pea and #FemkuMag, and a Feature Columnist for whiptail journal. Her debut e-chapbook, "I Am", was published by Title IX Press (now Moth Orchid Press) in 2019 and her second chapbook "Alone, I Am Not", was published by Velvet Dusk Publishing in April 2022.

VIDISHA KAUSHAL

Vidisha Kaushal is a granddaughter of fourth generation army officer and a Personal Development & Mindfulness Coach. An MBA from the UK, she has worked with some of the largest organizations and corporate giants in India and in the UK. She's featured on BBC Hindi, Radio Mirchi, Times of India and many international media houses. She is a global mediation master on the thinkright.me app. Her sessions and motivational talks have been rolled out across organisations and forums around the globe and are known to be interactive, thought-provoking & inspiring. She specializes in Mindfulness practices and Sound Healing & inspires people through her social media channels on a consistent basis.

VINITA NARULA

Dr. Vinita Narula W/O a colonel of Indian Army is a doting mother and grandmother. She is a former associate professor and vice principal of Lady Irwin College, Delhi University, she is credited with 44 years of teaching and administrative experience. Besides innumerable academic publications, she has been both on television and radio for academic presentations and discussions. She is extensively travelled, throughout the world, is positively engrained and full of life. She is a motivator who brings a smile to all and sundry through community work. Her new found love is the literary world and is penning down her thoughts and experiences both in prose and poetry. She has already contributed to over a dozen anthologies and takes a place of pride at poetic renditions especially as a life time achievement award by the iconic international poetry group "The Significant League," her maiden poetry book *Images* has been the Amazon best seller.

YASEEN MOHAMMED

Yaseen Mohammed is serving officer in Indian Navy and started writing poems in 2021. Hindi poems of various subjects interest him. However, he also does write and read English poetry.

VINOD KUMAR PANT

He is a serving Army Officer, commissioned in Jun 1992, Ex NDA 79th Course, Delta Squadron. His has Hobby of writing poems in Hindi, published one composition of Hindi Poems titled "Bhav avam Vichaar". Been serving in various locations and numerous army operations in various modes, he have been on deputation with Ministry of Civil Aviation and Special Forces Command as Armament and Ammunition Technical Officer. He is a double MBA (from Rani Durga Vati University, Jabalpur, MP and Mahrishi Dayanand University, Haryana) and M Sc (Munitions Technology) from RDVU, Jabalpur MP.

VIVEK KAMTHAN

He has passed out Engineering from Dayalbagh Educational Institute and MBA from FMS Delhi University. Joined IAF in 1993 and retired from AFS Faridabad as CEO of a Logistics Base of IAF, Spent around 26 years in IAF as Engineering Officer. Had experience of Fighter ac, Helicopter and UAV. He also flew around 1200 hours as Flight Engineer in MI class helicopter and participated in Kargil War for which he was awarded Mention-in-Dispatches. His interests lies in writing stories and poetry. His genre in stories is paranormal. He has written few novellas and now planning to publish them. He does poetry in Hindi as well as English and prefer to write humour and on Armed Forces.